Integrated Office System Planning Process

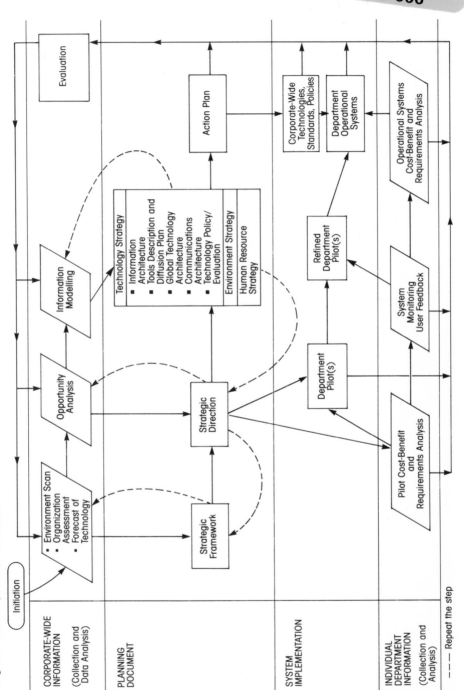

11903121

Planning
For
Integrated
Office
Systems

A STRATEGIC APPROACH

CONVERGING TECHNOLOGIES

Planning
For
Integrated
Office
Systems

A STRATEGIC APPROACH

TAPSCOTT, HENDERSON, AND GREENBERG
OF TRIGON SYSTEMS GROUP INC.

DOW JONES-IRWIN
HOMEWOOD, ILLINOIS 60430

Published by Holt, Rinehart and Winston of Canada, Limited
Published simultaneously in the USA by Dow Jones-Irwin, Inc.,
1818 Ridge Road, Homewood, Illinois 60430

ISBN 0-87094-6536

Library of Congress Catalog Card No. 84-72805

Printed in Canada

Special thanks to Don Tapscott, consulting editor and international authority in the field of integrated office systems.

Acknowledgements

This book could not have been written a year earlier. Because the topic is so new, it was necessary to acquire sufficient actual experience in building plans to be able to write something reasonably comprehensive. For this reason, we owe a great debt to two groups of people.

First are the clients of Trigon Systems Group Inc. As Trigon principals and before that managers of the integrated office systems consulting and research program at Bell Northern Research Ltd., we have been working with a variety of organizations since 1978 in planning for these new systems. The innovativeness, foresight, difficulties and successes of these clients have been the source of our knowledge about building strategic plans for this new generation of systems.

Second, we are deeply grateful to our colleagues at Trigon, and its sister company Emerald City Research Inc., who have toiled, often until the wee hours of the morning, forging strategies for our clients to take advantage of the new opportunities. The fruits of their work, insights and wisdom are presented in this book.

A number of other people helped us get this book on the mark. We thank Dr. Joe Arbuckle of Imperial Oil for his insightful views in early stages of development of the book. We received detailed and extremely useful comments on the manuscript by several very knowledgeable people — Bill Jarvis of the Labatts Brewing Company, Dean Meyer of Dean Meyer and Associates, Don Sheppard of the Imperial Bank of Commerce, and Paul Strassman of Xerox Corporation. Our thinking on several critical parts of the book was changed through the active involvement of David Ticoll of Trigon. Other colleagues, too numerous to mention, provided us with important insights on various chapters. Naturally, however, it is the authors who must take responsibility for the contents of the final manuscript.

We are also grateful for the technical consultation and assistance in the book's production by Ingrid Lebolt from Emerald City Research Inc., Laura Oda and Kathy Tapscott, both of Trigon.

We would like to give special thanks to our publisher Holt, Rinehart and Winston, and Ingrid Philipp Cook, the editor assigned to work with us. As a neophyte to the topic she, over a period of eighteen months, asked questions; pointed to inconsistencies; insisted on clarification; helped us reorganize the manuscript (several times); and did a detailed and rigorous edit. We appreciate her persistence and overall, invaluable contribution.

Finally, we would like to dedicate this book to our families and friends, in appreciation of their patience and understanding.

Contents

INTRODUCTION

Introduction

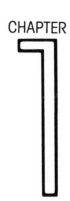

Since the beginning of the 1980s the productivity spotlight in the industrialized West has been on the office. While significant changes will happen in the plant — in particular through robotics and CAD/CAM (Computer Aided Design/Computer Aided Manufacturing) — the much-heralded "information technology" is having its greatest impact in the office.

The advent of the personal computer and the convergence of traditional computer, telecommunications, and office technologies has brought with it the new integrated office systems. More and more, all categories of officeworkers are being directly supported by the new multifunction workstations. Everyone from secretaries to CEO's is using these desktop computers or computer terminals, networked to other facilities, to improve information handling, communications, decisionmaking, time management and text authoring, in particular — and office administration and the quality of work life in general.

In many ways, the success of organizations over the next critical period will depend on how well they can make the turn and respond to the important changes now taking place. As various opportunities proliferate throughout organizations, a number of vital questions are being posed. For example:

- What changes should we make to our organizational structure?
- How much will it cost us to take advantage of the new technologies over a certain number of years?
- What are the long-range implications of selecting a pilot vendor in the short term?
- What is the likely impact of integrated office systems on the people who work with them?
- How do we develop a technology strategy to facilitate the integration of computer, communications and office technologies?
- What policies should we adopt to avoid problems and take full advantage of the proliferation of personal computers?

- What new business objectives can we undertake through use of the new technologies?
- How do we protect our investment in technology and position ourselves to evolve towards fully integrated systems?
- What strategy should we adopt for local area networks?
- How should we go about determining our requirements for systems in specific organizational units?
- What general evaluation plan should we put in place?
- How do we assess the likely impacts of the system on other areas such as physical plant, office space planning, lighting, acoustical requirements, and furniture?
- How can we ensure that our plans for implementation are consistent with our strategic direction?

Overall, the main issue is one of developing a coherent and comprehensive plan to drive the acquisition and use of the new technologies as well as to manage the organizational transformations being precipitated by these technologies.

There has been much discussion on the necessity of grappling with these issues, but, to date, little has been done towards developing effective methods of strategic planning for the new business environment. Office automation conferences of the 1970s and many through today, tried to fill the vacuum with such presentations as "Strategic Planning for the New Systems". However, the actual presentations too often had little to do with the title and tended to focus on system selection or implementation — to the great frustration of the executives in attendance. Time and again they were promised a planning boudoir, only to find themselves in an empty room.

The poverty of ideas from leaders in the field has reflected an underlying problem. The new planning methods we have been waiting for could not be developed in the universities or the labs. They had to germinate and grow in real organizations attempting to plan for and implement the new technologies.

The fact that this period was also one of major technological innovation further complicated the problem. The early 1980s was the dawn of the business microcomputer, the integrated private branch exchange (PBX) telephone system, the local area network (LAN), videotex, the multifunction workstation, and voice messaging, to name a few of these innovations. Building a technology strategy in such a volatile situation was next to impossible. This was also a period when most large organizations implemented their first integrated system pilots and began to grapple with the human, social, organizational, environmental and business implications of the new office technologies.

To be perfectly frank about it, strategic planning for integrated systems is *still* difficult, because of the constantly changing environment in which business must operate. But, at least, after some considerable experience and a picture of where the technology is headed, we can say that it is now possible, indeed essential. Without a strategic approach you will have planning by default — the technological imperative.

This book explains how to determine the Strategic Framework and Direction that will allow you to use the new integrated office systems to their full potential. It then explores the strategies and policies that can help ensure the prosperity of your enterprise in the coming years.

The Importance of Planning for Integrated Office Systems

It is sometimes fashionable, especially in turbulent and difficult times to argue that planning is a waste of time and often counterproductive. No less of an authority than management theorist Henry Mintzberg has warned against the dangers of taking a too formal and structured approach to planning. He argues that while strategists and planners are "scouring the corporate horizon for textbook cash cows, tomorrow's winning ways are probably emerging like weeds in the garden."[1]

The cry against planning has also been taken up in office automation and computer systems circles. Many so-called leaders in the field, intimidated by scope of the problem, confused by its complexity and frightened by the pitfalls have concluded that the best approach to these new technologies is the sink-or-swim method, or "bottom-up groping".

While there is much to be said for encouraging experimentation, initiatives and involvement from the bottom, no serious senior manager can turn his or her back on the challenge of planning for integrated systems. Strategic planning is critical to successful use of the new technologies for a number of reasons that are closely related to the critical questions posed at the beginning of this chapter.

1. The Scope of Integrated Systems
The new systems are much greater in scope than traditional computer, office or telecommunications systems. Because they have a social and environmental, as well as a technological component, they deeply and profoundly affect the nature of the organization. Planning is essential to ensure that changes required to all three components of the work system

are anticipated, and that all three are combined in the best manner or "jointly optimized" for maximum organizational performance.

2. The Costs of Technology

The transition from the manual to the electronic office involves huge capital expenditures and operating expenses. Some estimates indicate that one-third of the total capital costs of North American business will be spent on this technology over the next period. The sheer magnitude of such costs argues strongly for proper planning.

3. Protecting the Corporate Investment

Office technology is a moving target. It is unlikely to settle down for some time and we can expect to see major, significant advances continuing well into the next century. Moreover, the nature of development is evolutionary. Unlike traditional data processing, telephone or word processing systems, it is impossible to implement a complete, operational system for the organization all at once. In addition, much of the new technology is within the budgets of individual user groups. As individual user departments make independent purchases of equipment, the likelihood of creating obstacles to downstream integration increases. To protect corporate investments in technology, a plan is required whereby purchases will position the organization to evolve towards integrated systems. For example, a plan can channel the purchase of desktop computers by various departments into a direction which will make the best use of those computers within the corporate system as a whole.

4. The Complexity of the Technology

The new technologies are complex — much more so than the computer, office and telecommunications technologies which gave birth to these new systems. A plan is necessary to create a coherent technology strategy, whereby the various pieces of technology can come together for maximum impact on organizational performance. For example, an electronic mail system which enables employees with workstations to use it throughout the corporation will have a far greater impact than a system which, through lack of planning, is restricted to a certain user group. Or worse, lack of planning has often resulted in an organization's having several incompatible messaging systems in operation. Another example is the issue of planning access to corporate databases. A plan can enable technical interfaces with databases to be built.

5. The Issue of Responsibility

For each of the three technologies — computers, telecommunications, and the office — there is often an organizational counterpart in large organizations. Computing resources are managed by a person with a title such as Vice President of Electronic Data Processing or Management Information systems. Office technologies often fall under the Vice President of Administration or Finance. Telecommunications technologies may be planned by a Director of Corporate Telecommunications. Other senior managers may feel that they have a direct role to play in planning for and implementing the new systems. Good examples are executives of Human Resource Management, Corporate Planning and often the managers in charge of various other line and staff functions who feel that they should be responsible for new systems within their organizations. Sorting out who should drive the train and what should be the roles and responsibilities of the various stakeholders requires planning.

6. The Problem of Differing Perspectives

Office systems are still in their early stages and within organizations there are widely divergent views regarding the technology, the opportunities and how to take advantage of them. This is generally true across senior management, and also throughout the organization.

As a result, an office systems planning *process* is as important as the *plan* itself. This process requires various planners to come together and, hopefully, through a process of discovery, learning, debate and discussion, to crystallize their views around a common perspective and approach to the new systems. Sometimes differences are due not only to differing perspectives but also to differing *interests*. Office systems planning can often bring issues of turn and power to the fore. In the long run, a resolution of such disputes is necessary to realize the full potential of the technology to improve organizational performance. As we will see in Chapter Three, if handled properly, the planning process can raise and clarify the issues of differing perspectives and interests and facilitate their resolution.

7. The Issue of Managing Change

Traditionally, users of computer systems were computer experts. Most of those who will use the new systems know little about computers — nor should they. The advent of the non-technical user has affected many aspects of product design and implementation strategy. Manufacturers learned that to succeed they had to develop "friendly" systems, which were easy to use. The first of these were the Xerox Star and Apple's Lisa. In organizations, implementors also found that old approaches to installing systems did not work. New approaches to managing change which included comprehensive educational, training and support programs were required.

Planning is critical to the management of change and the diffusion of this major technological innovation throughout the organization. An over-all plan ensures that the users can be approached with clarity, consistency and authority. It also makes possible forecasting and planning for the implementation resources which will be required.

8. The Growing Demands for Technology

With the onslaught of the business microcomputer and the first successful office system pilots in organizations, a "contagion phenomenon" has developed in which "everybody wants one". Such pressures for systems create the danger of everyone going off in a different direction. Planning is required to properly channel such enthusiasm and, at the same time, manage expectations of the potential users.

9. Opportunity Management

By solving old problems in new ways, the steam and internal combustion engines created entirely new industries and services. The same thing is now happening with information technologies. Successful organizations — in all sectors of the economy — are devising new products, services and management systems. By redefining its business objectives while taking account of the new technologies, an organization can position itself to survive and succeed in the coming years.

A Comprehensive Planning Method

The objective of this book is to provide a strategic approach to planning for integrated systems. There are no magic recipes for integrating office systems. (Wouldn't it be nice if there were? Take one mainframe, add one micro for each employee, mix with integrated software and plug in.) However, the analytic framework we have developed will allow your organization and its own advisers to build and execute a plan for integrated systems that is firmly grounded in the enterprise's own realities.

Each chapter discusses an important topic that must be investigated in planning for integrated systems. In other words, each chapter explores a component of an integrated systems plan — indeed many plans we have helped develop contain a section corresponding to a chapter of this book. We end with a synthesis of the planning issues, showing how systems and plans evolve, and making some projections for the future.

The relationship between main components of a complete integrated systems plan are illustrated and explained in Figure 1.1. It shows:

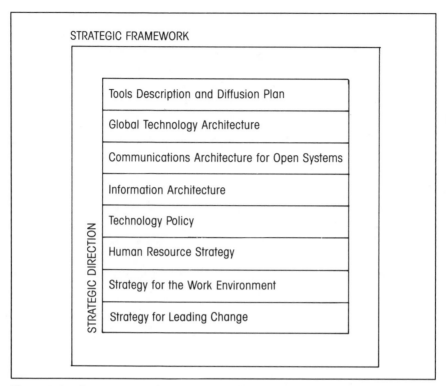

STRATEGIC FRAMEWORK

Tools Description and Diffusion Plan

Global Technology Architecture

Communications Architecture for Open Systems

Information Architecture

Technology Policy

Human Resource Strategy

Strategy for the Work Environment

Strategy for Leading Change

STRATEGIC DIRECTION

Figure 1.1 Components of an Integrated Systems Plan

- the **Strategic Framework** which is an assessment of the context within which the organization finds itself
- the **Strategic Direction** for which the organization will use the new technologies to meet business and organizational objectives and to enable those objectives to evolve
- a **Tools Description and Diffusion Plan** outlining what corporate-wide tools will be provided across the organization and how these will be sequenced or phased
- a **Global Technology Architecture** structuring how computer intelligence and databases will be distributed across the organization
- a **Communications Strategy for Open Systems** which will enable the enterprise to grow into an "open system", multivendor environment where devices are fully compatible
- an **Information Architecture** based on information modeling to establish how data will be distributed to serve user needs
- a **Technology Policy** which can give direction and leadership to various line and user departments in the area of technology but which

does not restrict them unnecessarily in areas which are best handled at the departmental level

- a **Human Resource Strategy** to prepare for and manage the important changes required in the composition, skills and knowledge of your computerized organization
- a **Strategy for the Work Environment** which will enable the physical plant of the organization to evolve in harmony with the rest of the system
- a **Strategy for Leading Change**, enabling appropriate education, training and leadership in implementing a short-term Action Plan.

The reader will see from this outline that strategic planning for integrated systems is a somewhat complex undertaking, which requires considerable effort and resources. However, with organizational performance, productivity, quality of work life and in many ways, the success and survival of your organization on the line over the next period, the stakes are high. The lessons in this book, if heeded, should help your organization and the people in it to be winners.

PLANNING FOR INTEGRATED OFFICE SYSTEMS:

The Promise and the Challenge

The Promise of Integrated Office Systems

The "office of the future" will, by definition, never arrive. In the middle and late 1970s, the term was used by everyone from word-processing vendors to furniture manufacturers to generate interest in the changes taking place in the office. No one could really define this "future" office, but as the excitement grew, it didn't really matter.

The momentum behind the "office of the future" movement came from two fundamental sources. The first was the growing need for improved productivity in the office. This became known as the "demand pull". The second was a "technology push" caused by a number of significant developments in technology.

Demand Pull

The most commonly used argument for investment in office technology goes something like this:

> The average capital expenditure per factory worker is $30,000. Industrial productivity has increased 100 percent during the last 10 years. The average capital expenditure per officeworker is $2,000. Office productivity has increased 4 percent during the same period. Therefore, if capitalization of the office is increased similar productivity improvements can be realized. [1]

This analogy is indeed wrong on several counts.

- Most costs in the office are recorded as "expense" rather than as "capital acquisition." The figure of $2,000 per worker is a misleading measure of how much is spent per officeworker. Moreover, such figures overlook costs of office buildings and other major expenditures for the office. The fact is that the cost per officeworker is large.
- While technology in the plant often supports improved output, its main function is to *replace* workers. This cost-displacement model works poorly in the office where work is less structured.
- It was ambitious, to say the least, to have estimated increases in office productivity over the last ten years. Measuring office productivity, even in

an individual site, has proven to be no simple business. Such estimations on a national scale are pretty meaningless.

• While technology may have improved productivity greatly in the factory, it is wrong to assume that its impact will automatically be the same in the office. Since the office is a much more complex place than the plant, the nature of the technology, the climate for change, the implementation process and other variables deeply affect whether improvements are realized.

Despite the problems with the popular analogy, there is a clear need to improve organizational performance in the white collar sector. That sector of the economy is growing, and is now a majority of the workforce in western industrialized countries. However, this is not to say we are moving towards a purely "information economy" as some have argued. [2]

A society cannot eat, wear or be sheltered by information. As a result, industrial production is still, and will continue to be, the backbone of western economies. However, as production, the economy, and social organization become more complex, the role of information becomes more pervasive. So, the role of technology becomes more critical.

Take the example of the telephone system. It has been estimated that without modern switching technology half of the entire U.S. workforce would have to work at plug boards just to switch telephone traffic.

Similarly, modern technology was needed to handle the complexities of scheduling and reservations which accompanied the growth of the commercial aviation industry. As business transactions increased in volume and complexity, various types of technology were required — from traditional data processing for payroll and accounting to special systems to coordinate traffic lights.

Technology Push

Coincidental with, and in many ways contributing to the "demand pull", has been a push towards integrated office systems as a result of several major technological innovations.

First is the chip. Tales of the chip have become commonplace. For example, in 1950 the largest computer filled an entire floor of an office building. It required tons of air-conditioning equipment to cool the vacuum tubes and it broke down every minute or so. Today, that same amount of computer power is about half the size of your smallest fingernail and costs a few dollars. Moore's law states that the number of tiny components on a chip doubles every year — a law that has proven true over the past couple of decades. [3]

A discussion of microelectronics inevitably leads to a second analogy — the comparison between chip technology and automotive technology. It is said that if the automotive industry had progressed as rapidly as the chip industry, you could buy a Cadillac today for fifty dollars. It would travel at 5,000 miles per hour and its fuel consumption would be 2,000 miles per gallon.

But ask yourself, what would you do with a car that could travel that fast? What roads would support it? What skills would be required to drive it? How many would be available at that price? What would be the impact on ecology, city life, and human safety?[4] Many people are beginning to ask similar questions about the new technologies.

Nevertheless, the chip is creating processing power at a cost which is making it possible to directly support every officeworker with powerful new tools.

Related to the rise of the chip have been a number of historic developments in telecommunications. The growth of local and wide area networks is enabling the transmission of voice, data, text and graphic information across the office, into homes and around the world.

The new networks have their origins in a number of areas. The common carriers have developed wide area networks for switching all kinds of information all over the globe. The major computer manufacturers have developed computer communications networks for exchange of data locally between devices and, through attachment to common carrier networks, across wide areas. The telephone equipment manufacturers have developed private branch exchanges (PBXs) which route not only voice, but other kinds of information in the office. The cable companies have moved beyond providing one-way television to homes to providing interactive technologies such as videotex. Specialized network suppliers have entered into the fray, providing local area networks (LANs), satellite networks, microwave networks and cellular radio networks, to name a few.

A third significant technological development pushing us towards integrated systems is the convergence of three traditional technologies:

- **computer technologies** of data processing (DP) or management information systems (MIS);
- **office technologies** such as typing devices, photocopiers, and microform; and
- **telecommunications technologies** such as telephones, telex and PBXs.

These three technologies are converging to a point where it is difficult to discuss them separately. Figure 2.1 shows how these technologies have converged over the past four decades. During the 1950s electromechanical devices reigned supreme. The 1960s brought the development of the electronic PBX, photocopiers and electronic typewriters and electronic data processing (EDP). The 1970s saw the advent of the digital PBX and packet switching, word processing and management information systems. In the 1980s the main theme has been *integration*, with the integrated voice and data PBX, "interconnect" and LANs, office automation, and the concept of information resource management (IRM). In the office, these have converged to bring us the electronic workstation. The future is bringing us the new integrated communication information systems. These systems integrate technology throughout the organization, combining factory production systems, process control, transaction systems like automatic teller machines (ATMs) or specialized technologies like CAD/CAM with the integrated office systems discussed in this book.

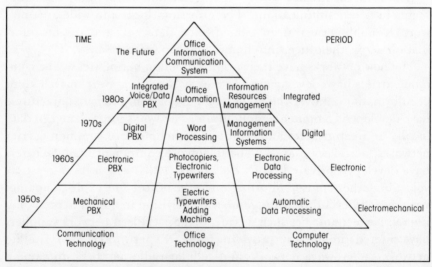

Figure 2.1   Evolution of Office Technologies

Tools of the Electronic Workstation

Before launching into our discussion of planning for integrated office systems, it is essential that you have a clear understanding of what these systems are and of how they are fundamentally different from traditional technologies in the office.

With the exception of the telephone, traditional office technologies did not affect most office personnel in a direct or substantial way. It is true that some clerical employees were displaced by traditional data processing. However, data processing, and even its extension into management information systems, has not fundamentally altered the way that most people work in the office. Similarly, traditional word processing was used only by secretaries and operators and its impact on the enterprise and people in the office was limited.

The coming together of traditional computer, office and telecommunications technologies is changing the picture profoundly. The central product of this convergence is the personal, electronic workstation, as shown in figure 2.2. Like the transition from the hoe to the tractor or the hammer to the assembly line, the impact on both productivity and the nature of work is dramatic.

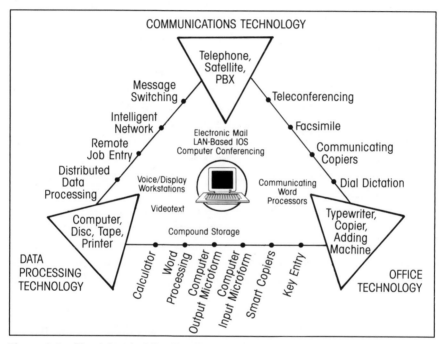

Figure 2.2   The Advent of the Electronic Workstation

Multifunction workstations — in the form of a microcomputer or computer terminal — provide a number of tools which can be used directly by all types of office personnel. These tools are integrated together to provide a whole which is much greater than the sum of its parts.

They are also becoming easier to use. Traditional computer systems were designed for highly technical people, who were familiar with "computerese," complicated interaction routines, system commands and responses like "system dead," "kill," "execute," "abort," or "illegal entry" (a criminal offense in most countries). This type of "user interface" presented an obstacle to computer use by non-programmers.

As word processors and office systems based on large computers began to make their appearance, designers attempted to create "friendly" interfaces. So the end-user was often subjected to such pseudo-human responses as "Good morning Bob. And how are you today?", or "Lovely day isn't it?", which were programmed into the system. Of course the computer was oblivious to the fact that there was a hail storm outside, and what once seemed "friendly" soon became just silly.

A second new approach to interface design was the creation of "icons", or pictorial images of office materials like a file folder, wastepaper basket or filing cabinet on the screen. Products such as the Xerox Star and the Apple Lisa and Macintosh were partial steps forward. However, the early implementations of the concept were often flawed, resulting in users "losing" pieces of paper under others on the screen and similar problems.

The clear direction for the future is to design interfaces which are as transparent as water. As computer designer Ted Nelson has explained, an interface should also be intuitive, as for example in a video game. The end-user should be able to sit down at a new workstation and begin to use it without the aid of a huge, intimidating training manual.

Different employees may have workstations which provide different tools. While some may use certain tools more than others, many tools are used by just about everyone in the office. So most of the better integrated system workstations provide the same "big six" groups of functions: communications, information handling, decision support, document preparation and presentation, time management and system administration.

It should be noted that there are as many ways of grouping office systems tools as there are possible permutations and combinations. However, the groupings described here are probably the most useful.

Communications Tools

Because managers and many other employees spend most of their time in some form of communication activity, electronic tools which can address such activities can have an important impact.

There are two main types of communications tools. Non-simultaneous (asynchronous) tools allow the initiation and receipt of the communication to take place at different times — like an electronic post office. On the other hand, simultaneous (or synchronous) tools improve or enable immediate communications between the initiator and one or more receivers, as in a telephone conversation. Simultaneous tools also permit people to work on the same document at the same time.

One of the earliest non-simultaneous tools was *electronic document distribution*, or as it is sometimes called, "communicating word-processing." This tool distributes documents at the speed of light rather than at the speed of the post office or internal mail system. It also provides a permanent electronic record of documents which can be searched by subject, author, keyword or date.

Text and voice messaging are also non-simultaneous tools which are quite different in their features and underlying functions from document distribution. These two tools address problems with telephone or face-to-face communications and also with short notes or memos. Such problems center on "shadow functions" or unplanned activities in the communications process which have no value. Examples are telephone "tag" where I'm out when you call and vice versa; calls to busy numbers; calls to "black holes" where the phone keeps ringing and ringing; and journeys down the hall looking for a colleague.

With the help of a good text messaging system a person can to compose and send messages quickly, using simple commands such as compose, reply, forward, file, send and delete. The system provides for automatic addressing, use of distribution lists, creation of various folders for filing mail, annotation of messages and it even recognizes nicknames. A full-feature messaging system has several dozen capabilities which can be acquired over time and, if well integrated with the rest of the system, will allow output from an electronic spreadsheet, for example, to be inserted in a message. Without these attributes, users will continue to use the telephone and traditional communications modes.

Voice messaging addresses similar problems to text messaging, and so such systems have many of the same features as their text messaging counterparts — only the communication medium is voice. Each has advantages or disadvantages, depending on the user and type of use.

Computer conferencing, not to be confused with teleconferencing, is another form of non-simultaneous communications tool. A computer conference is basically a written meeting. A user scans through summaries of the "meetings" he or she is currently attending, selects a meeting, reads all the latest comments, makes his or her own contribution to the conference, and so on. More sophisticated computer conferencing systems permit you to make blind "asides" to limited groups of people, have a chairperson to lead the conference discussion, initiate sub-conferences (branching) and take votes at various points (balloting). The benefits and challenges of computer conferences have been well documented in works such as *The Network Nation* by Hiltz and Turoff and *Electronic Meetings* by Johansen, Vallee and Spangler.

Computer conferencing eliminates the two main problems of time and geography. People no longer all have to be at the same place at the same time to have a meeting. It is also useful in clarifying issues or the agenda *in advance of* a face-to-face meeting. As well, a written record of the computer "meeting" can be useful for production of reports, or for later reference.

Teleconferencing is a form of simultaneous communications which is becoming more widespread and sophisticated. In the simplest case, more than two persons hold a "telephone meeting". More advanced (and expensive) forms of teleconferencing include "slow scan", where "frames" of visual information supplement the audio conference, through to full video conferencing, in which participants see a live video of all or part of the group.

The main advantages of teleconferencing are not only the cost reduction and avoidance of travel expenses (particularly routine or administrative travel), but the value-added benefits of encouraging geographically dispersed persons to meet when travel is not feasible.

Shared workspace conferencing is a form of simultaneous communications, where more than one participant is viewing "live" information on a screen while conducting an audio teleconference. Two executives, for example, can be examining the latest sales figures and asking "what-if questions" while discussing the material before them over the telephone. A shared workspace is also useful as a substitute for single-issue, face-to-face meetings which require travel or even for ad hoc meetings on a given topic for participants in close geographical proximity.

Enhanced telephony refers to the broad selection of telephone tools provided by the new digital PBXs or key telephone sets. These tools improve both simultaneous and non-simultaneous communications, cutting costs, saving time, and augmenting human interaction. For example, a PBX can: automatically re-dial a busy number; find a number in a corporate directory; forward your calls to another location; advise you when it has successfully placed a call; enable audio conferencing; and store and forward voice messages. Literally hundreds of features are available, which if appropriately selected and used, can be very beneficial. The direction has been established that the telephone set is not a separate device, but part of the workstation.

Information-Handling Tools

While, in a sense, all the functions of a workstation assist in handling information, the device can provide a number of capabilities specifically oriented to providing better access to, and management of, information in databases.

Electronic filing and retrieval tools help each end-user store and access information — not only in textual form but also for the media of data, voice, and image. Typically such tools are used to file text documents, and text and voice messages. Files can be grouped in electronic folders, drawers and filing cabinets.

The workstation can also provide *access to corporate databases*. The end-user, rather than wading through a thick printout from the enterprise's computer, can work directly on the screen with the centralized database. Thus the management information systems (MIS) of the 1970s are becoming the interactive databases of the 1980s.

In addition to corporate information, the workstation can enable *access to external databases* — the publically available world of computerized information. Public networks, such as the telephone system, can be used to connect to and interact with information ranging from stock quotations, libraries, online newspaper records, and airline schedules to the weather report in Singapore or hog prices in Chicago.

The introduction of the corporate microcomputer also made it possible for users to construct *personal or local databases* on their own desktop, or within their work group. For example, the education co-ordinator may construct a local database on public educational seminars, so that he can answer queries in this area. A salesperson may build a local database on prospects and contacts.

The trend in all such cases is away from traditional database formats to "relational" databases where data elements are differently structured and much more easily accessible.

In general, these information-handling tools contribute to the realization of the time-honored goal of getting the right information to the right people at the right time, in a cost-effective manner. When properly designed and implemented, these tools can help improve many aspects of decisionmaking that involve the use of information.

Document Preparation and Presentation Tools

Word processing spearheaded much of the movement towards integrated office systems in the 1970s. Originally conceived as a tool to improve typing efficiency, the focus has shifted towards using word processing to enhance the creativity of the writer.

Text editors and formatters not only eliminate retyping but also provide powerful tools to assist an author in structuring his or her thoughts and getting those ideas down. When word processing first became widespread, the thought of a professional or manager using the tool directly was almost heretical. However, the popularity of the personal computer, combined with the growing functionality and simplicity of office systems, has inspired people to take advantage of the new opportunities. The common phrase is: "I don't type but I can keyboard forty words a minute."

One of the most useful word-processing features is *list processing*. The ability to construct and administer lists, such as mailing lists, was an early feature of word-processing systems. However, with integrated systems, list-processing capabilities are integrated with other tools, dramatically increasing their utility. For example, it is possible to select names from a client database which meet certain criteria and send each a customized form letter.

Document design tools such as spelling and grammar checkers are becoming increasingly popular. When Xerox introduced the Star workstation in the late 1970s, it was a quantum leap in text management systems. The Star (or 9100 as it became called) offered a choice of text type in various styles and sizes and its paper output was almost identical to what appeared on the screen. High resolution graphics, scientific notation and other advanced features could be integrated with text for the first time. The Star also popularized the "mouse" — which had been shown in lab studies to be a more efficient cursor-control device than traditional pointers.

Decision Support Tools

Decision support tools, as they have become known, help in making decisions that involve the use and analysis of numbers.

The simplest tool is an *online calculator*. More advanced are the *electronic spreadsheets* that have become very popular for personal computers. The first was Visicalc, followed by enhanced look-alikes such as Supercalc and Multiplan, followed in turn by software packages which integrated more sophisticated spreadsheets with other capabilities, such as Lotus 1-2-3 (and its successor Symphony), Context MBA, Framework and VisiOn. Such tools enable a manager, for example, to construct a complex budget spreadsheet. He or she can change variables or entries in the budget and instantly see the effects on other numbers in the budget.

More powerful, yet more difficult to use, *modeling tools* had been around on the market for some time prior to this. Some of the earliest were the Interactive Financial Planning System (IFPS) and Empire.

Lacking some of the data-manipulating capabilities of the spreadsheets and financial planning tools, but having far superior statistical capabilities, are the *statistical analysis tools*.

Packages such as the Statistical Package for the Social Sciences (SPSS) were introduced in the 1960s. As online versions became available, the feasibility of integrating these into a workstation was recognized, and soon accomplished.

As these tools become widely used, the research evidence indicates dramatic time savings, reduction in error rate, more sensitive financial plans, and a better quality of decisions. In any case, faced with the momentum of user enthusiasm, it is really a case of "You don't need a weatherman to know which way the wind blows." Decision support tools have proven themselves, and the productivity impact, while hard to measure, is clear.

Time and Resource Management Tools

A fifth important category of tools assists with the management of personal time and resources. *On-line calendars* were slow to find acceptance due to their lack of portability and to the fact that most calendars were rudimentary and awkward. However, as systems improved, the advantages of such tools became more widely known.

Entries in an electronic calendar become entries in a *diary* database which can be searched by date, or name, or combination of attributes. A good calendaring system also enables the construction and management of *to-do lists, reminders and ticklers*. Such tools can be customized to the wishes of the user. For example, items "to do" can be automatically forwarded to the next day if they're not completed.

One of the most important time management tools is electronic *meeting scheduling*. Again, this feature took a while to get off the ground, primarily because of resistance to electronic diaries and also the fact that there wasn't a fully usable meeting scheduling system on the market until 1984. With a good system, the user can request a meeting of all the people in her department and the system will (among other things):

- Automatically search all calendars to find an available time
- Automatically send a message to this list of people requesting a meeting
- Automatically schedule the meeting for everyone once the meeting time has been confirmed.

One of the difficulties with meeting scheduling tools is that their successful use requires some significant changes in office procedures. For example, it requires that all users maintain an electronic diary. It also requires agreement among users regarding who can schedule a meeting for whom. Because the resolution of such human and organizational issues tends to lag behind the maturity of the technology, it is understandable that meeting scheduling has yet to achieve its full potential.

Project management tools were developed in the traditional data-processing environment, particularly for engineering and software development. More recently there has been a trend to apply project management methods to a wide range of projects in the office. However no project management tools were integrated into office systems until 1983. The first such user-friendly tool was introduced as part of Apple's Lisa. Although the tool had some considerable weaknesses, its links to project-flow graphics and its "what if" capabilities highlighted the utility of such tools for the first time.

In general, time and resource management tools have been shown to make striking reductions in the time spent in corresponding administrative activities. However, a major procedural change is required to take advantage of such opportunities.

System Administration and Other Tools

A variety of other tools provided by a workstation also deliver important functionality to the user and are critical to system success.

Help facilities get users out of trouble and assist them in learning the system. More sophisticated computer assisted learning (CAL) or computer assisted instruction (CAI) tools provide the new user with interactive, self-paced training. Such tools can also be used to teach office personnel other skills which may not be directly system-related.

System administration tools are essential for the system administrator, who may be a non-technical person, to set up user IDs and passwords, modify security levels, archive old files, do system back-ups, conduct system accounting for user billing, and other such activities.

Rather than being viewed as a major functional area (one of the "big six"), *business graphics* are best viewed as a tool which can augment many of the other tools. Graphic output from decision support tools became popular with the introduction of packages like Lotus 1-2-3. Graphic output from information-handling tools, such as corporate databases, enables complex corporate information to be easily assessed by senior management.

One important development here was the use of videotex (without a "t") to automatically generate graphic information from corporate databases. The North American Presentation Level Protocol Syntax (NAPLPS) code of videotex is basically a set of rules that allows numerical information to be translated into color videotex pictures. For years videotex was seen as a tool for "information providers" to sell information to "information users". However, as some of these providers introduced services which simply generated videotex from existing databases, such as the Dow Jones, corporate systems executives started to take note of the opportunity to do the same within their own organization.

Data-processing tools process structured information such as accounts payable, accounts receivable, general ledger and payroll. These workstation functions are especially important for small organizations.

As systems expand and are more fully integrated, we will see still further additions to these systems. Tools specific to a job type or vertical sector of the economy may provide the backbone of an integrated system. For the building maintenance personnel in a large office building or complex *energy management tools* may constitute an important part of the system. For the insurance actuary, custom *risk analysis tools* may be at the center of their workstation.

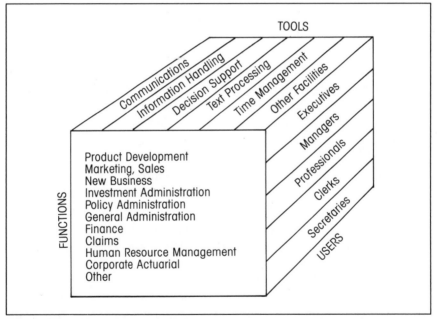

Figure 2.3   Tools, Users, and Functions

In summary then, an electronic workstation can provide a number of tools to directly support a wide range of officeworkers. An example from the insurance industry may help illustrate this. Figure 2.3 illustrates the key categories of tools, users, and functions within a typical insurance company.

Integration of Tools

The term "integration" has certainly been used frequently to describe the new technology. But what, really, does it mean? In fact, there are several levels of integration.[5]

- Integration of the **tools**, for example, *so information can be taken from a corporate* database; analyzed using a decision support tool; translated into graphic output; inserted into a text file; sent as a text message; with voice annotation on the message; and an automatic reminder going into a to-do list and tickler to follow up on the action item.
- Integration of the **media** of data, text, voice and image, resulting in the notion of the compound document.
- Integration **over distance**, so that the end-user can access the system from several locations.
- Integration **over time**, leading to systems that can be upgraded and so evolve.
- Integration **with other technologies in the office**, such as photocopier/printers, microform, telephone systems or the corporate mainframes.
- Integration with **the social and environmental components** of the overall work system, so that jobs, procedures, organizational structures and the physical environment are jointly optimized with the technology.
- Integration with **paper-based information systems** (which will be around for some time to come) so they can be managed and items found more easily.
- Integration of **the user interface** — the commands, graphics, format and language which stands between the person and the workstation. This integration reflects an underlying integrated software architecture enabling, for example, a universal presentation mode and consistent command syntax and semantics, where the word "read" means the same thing wherever you are in the system.

All these levels of integration must be considered as possible opportunities. To construct a technology strategy it is, not only necessary to specify the functionality or tools which will constitute the corporate-wide aspects of the office system, but also *the degree of functional integration between these tools.*

A case study will help clarify what we mean by integration of functional tools. Figure 2.4 illustrates the overall functional requirements identified in a large financial organization. As can be seen from the example, this organization had corporate-wide requirements for electronic

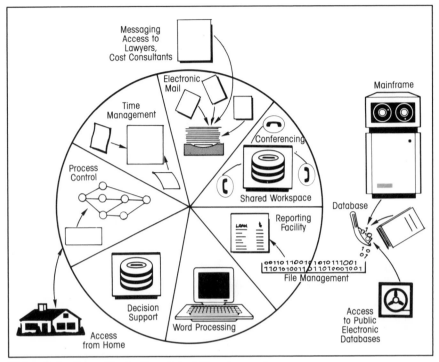

Figure 2.4 Case Study: Functional Requirements

mail, time management, teleconferencing, shared workspace, word processing, decision support, tracking and reporting of loan processes, file management, access to corporate databases and access to external public databases.

Figure 2.5 takes these functional requirements a step further and indicates the links, or areas where tools should be integrated to make the system fully usable and useful for this organization. In this case it was necessary, for example, to move information from the loan reporting facility, analyze it using a decision support tool, insert the results from that analysis in a word-processing document and hold a shared workspace teleconference with all parties simultaneously examining the same document.

So, unlike previous computer systems, the new generation of technologies: combine a number of tools together into an *integrated workstation* with a new focus of *directly supporting* most categories of people who work in the office in their structured *and* unstructured activities. The result is a far-reaching change in the nature of human work. If the technology is quite different from traditional systems, are the benefits or opportunities different as well?

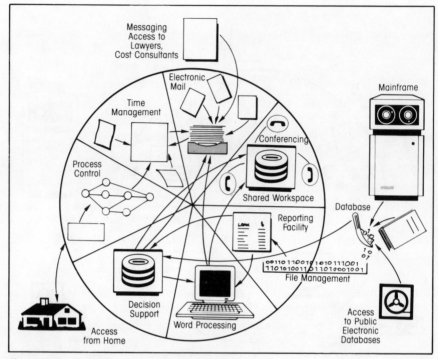

Figure 2.5 Case Study: Integration of Tools

Organizational Performance and the New Systems

As discussed at the outset of this chapter, few would dispute the need to increase productivity in the office. The recent recession brought this lesson home to most every executive suite in North America as business management searched for ways to cut costs, in particular to reduce personnel. However, there is less agreement over the question of how to measure productivity in the office. The industrial model of productivity (the ratio of output to input) works poorly in the office. Somehow an increase in office memos just doesn't sit well as a measure of productivity. Similarly, reductions in inputs such as managerial time savings can be less than convincing as arguments for investments in technology given Parkinson's and other laws. (Parkinson's law states that "work expands to fill the time available.")

Office work has traditionally been viewed as overhead. Consistent with this view, and with the immaturity of the technology, computers were applied to reduce office costs. The first wave of computers improved the efficient processing of structured data in the office (accounts, payroll, etc).

Word processing was introduced to improve typing efficiency. Transaction systems such as automatic teller machines were designed to cut office costs.

However, many project cost savings did not materialize. (Does your organization spend less on typing with word processing?) Moreover, many of the main benefits went beyond cost-displacement. For example, data processing led to management information systems. Word processing led to text editing tools for authors. Transaction systems are leading to electronic banking and the transformation of that industry.

As computer, telecommunications and office technologies converge and mature, their potential to directly and profoundly affect the less structured work of all office personnel up to the Chief Executive Officer is being revealed. And when office systems are linked to production and transaction systems, decisionmakers are put in closer touch with both their organizations and environment.

The point is that the new office systems don't simply reduce administrative costs, they enable people and organizations to do things in *new ways* and, with the reinvestment of saved time, to do *new things*.

Old notions of productivity must, therefore, give way to new approaches to improving *organizational performance*, in which the concept of *effectiveness* is added to the output/input equation.

As a result, the use of integrated systems is becoming an issue of *strategy* for many organizations. That is, the new technology is increasingly being viewed as a central and critical component of overall business strategy and the achievement of business goals. Indeed, successful diffusion of technological innovation in the office is becoming a prerequisite for business success and even survival.

Describing, let alone quantifying, the benefits of the new integrated systems is a tricky business. The benefits are complex, they overlap, and they are often somewhat intangible. Many a proposed pilot implementation or the extension of a pilot to a full operational system has been terminated by senior managers who were simply not presented with acceptable evidence of the benefits. For them, the costs were pretty straightforward, but not the benefits.

However, as the sophistication of methods for assessing opportunities grow, coupled with the office system success stories, the case is becoming stronger that the new systems can transform the performance of an organization by degrees which have been poorly understood in the past.

Clearly there are still significant opportunities to improve organizational efficiency through *cost displacement and cost avoidance*. Electronic workstations can produce savings in areas such as staff requirements, equipment, overtime, space and costs of materials. Utilization of plant and equipment can be improved through improved scheduling. Costs can also be reduced through workstation-based management of inventories, or plant and equipment utilization.

In the private sector such savings can provide a competitive edge by positioning the company for price leadership. Cost reduction and avoidance can also enable a tight ship in these times of troubled waters, as well as have a positive impact on profitability and the bottom line.

In the public sector, systems can be decisive in holding the line on cost increases and taxes while at the same time maintaining the quality of the public services or products being provided.

Integrated systems can also provide substantial *soft dollar* savings, which can be translated into "hard dollar" savings or improvements. The most common type of soft dollar improvement is time savings. A manager, for example, can typically save a significant proportion of the day if unplanned, useless activities — such as telephone tag, waiting for meetings to begin, waiting at the photocopier or for files — is reduced. Information seeking and gathering, writing, analyzing numbers and proofreading are tasks that can often be expedited, and completely inappropriate activities could be delegated to others if only those others had "more" time. Time savings can result in labor cost reduction, or, with a reinvestment strategy, in the undertaking of work that was not previously possible.

Through the reinvestment of saved time, an organization can generate better and different products. For example, time can be reinvested into better financial planning, better supervision of personnel, or better research into new opportunities. The technology can provide *added value* to existing products that may have had to compete in price alone. Large airlines such as American and United are getting the edge on competition by making travel agents reliant on airline information systems which, in subtle ways, may give preferential treatment.

The technology can also generate new information-based products and services. A striking example is the variety of computer-based financial products and services that the larger banks are beginning to offer to customers. Another is the insurance agent selling custom policies through a portable terminal, who has an obvious advantage over an agent with a pencil and paper.

Value can also be added through reducing product development lead times, improving the effective distribution of products and improving the responsiveness of the organization to new product opportunities. Customer-company relationships can be improved through a workstation, as in the cases of companies whose service, complaints or claims departments have online access to appropriate databases and people to solve customer problems and answer inquiries. The list goes on and on.

A fourth area of improvements can be called *qualitative improvements*. These less tangible benefits are difficult to quantify and even more different to assign a dollar value to, but have considerable importance. An integrated office system environment, for example, can increase the metabolism of the organization as documents begin to move at the speed of light, as text and voice messaging systems lead to fewer interruptions and as less time spent in waiting or looking for information.

A well-designed work system, of which the new technology is a key component, tends to go hand-in-hand with high quality of work life and high employee motivation. A company which uses the technology well can enhance its corporate image, gaining new markets and strong customer loyalty.

The bottom line, is that the new technology can itself impact the bottom line. This impact can be positive. It can also be negative. Which brings us back to the topic of planning.

The Changing Nature of Systems Planning

The new integrated office systems will require new approaches to systems planning. This fact has been overlooked by most detractors of planning for new office technologies. Charging unknowingly at the windmill of traditional methods of systems planning, opponents have argued that:

- Planning is undesirably exclusionary and undemocratic, prohibiting end-users, line management and non-technical senior managers — upon whom the future successful use of technology rests — from effective participation in the process.
- Planning is often used by data-processing managers — threatened by the growth of personal computers, word processing and the like — to bring the use of all technology back under their control. Worse, it is used to stop the implementation of non-traditional technologies.
- Planning represents the view that systems should be imposed from above, or implemented from the top down by a central systems authority.
- Planning is unrealistic. The technology is too complex to plan every detail. The technology is moving too fast to predict where it will go. Moreover, as the ink dries on the plan (or as it flashes off the laser printer) it will already be out of date.
- Because corporate-wide systems require significant financial and other resources, planning will tend to retard implementation and productivity improvement.

Many of these views grow out of bad experiences with a traditional systems planning. Traditional data processing (DP) or management information systems (MIS) often were owned and strictly controlled by the systems department, planned and implemented in a corporate-wide and top-down fashion, and designed by systems personnel with little input from the end-users. Frequently they were really strictly technology plans — lacking appreciation of the business context and the human and organizational implications of technology.

Autocratic approaches to planning are inappropriate to the new convergent technologies; but let's not throw out the whole idea of planning. Rather, the starting point in preparing for the new technologies and the new opportunities is a clear understanding of the changing nature of systems planning. From our experience in helping large and small organizations build integrated systems plans, it is evident that a number of trends are emerging. These trends reflect both the mistakes and successes of enterprises which have pioneered in harnessing the new technologies to achieve corporate objectives.

TREND: Systems strategy is converging with overall corporate business strategy

As technology becomes more important to the success and even survival of the enterprise, systems strategy becomes increasingly important to business strategy. In turn, a more strategic approach to planning for systems becomes necessary.

Computer systems planning was often done in a vacuum, isolated from the broader issues of business strategy. But good planners of traditional data-processing systems have always argued that a DP plan must be based on a clear strategic plan for the organization as a whole. How then is integrated systems planning different?

The scope and potential of the new converging technologies is so much broader than traditional systems, it will, in fact, have a direct and growing impact on the overall business plan. As the technologies mature and become more powerful and usable, they can open up vast new potential for the enterprise as a whole.

Take the financial services industry as an example. Banks, trust companies, insurance companies, securities companies and others are coming into direct competition with one another. This coming together of markets and objectives results from a number of factors, including changes in government regulations, saturated traditional markets, the considerable resources for expansion available to many of these companies, changes in public attitudes and the possibilities for new markets technology has opened up. One, and perhaps the main weapon in the coming epic battle is technology. Besides using integrated systems to deliver innovative services to new and existing customers, organizations can also use integrated systems to achieve new objectives. For example, one of our financial service clients succeeded in:

- freeing up marketing personnel to spend over 50 percent of their day in direct customer contact as opposed to the 7 percent of the day they used to spend;

- tripling the volume of loans processed with no increase in staff;
- managing their business more effectively despite its increasing complexity, so the organization can continue to function and respond quickly as a unit even as it expands regionally.

So while planning for integrated office systems and overall strategic business planning are, at present, separate activities, management must begin to forge links between the two. An understanding of the context or "Strategic Framework" within which the organization finds itself provides the foundation from which an overall direction for systems should be determined. Conversely, initial planning activities for the new systems can bring strategic business issues to the surface.

If your organization has a strategic business plan, then preparing for integrated systems will be that much easier, since much of your information will already have been collected. In turn the business plan may be modified in accordance with a deeper understanding, acquired through systems planning, of the strategic potential which the technology holds.

The reality is that most organizations do not have a formal strategic business plan. Most practice some financial planning, usually in the form of an annual budget. Some go beyond this to forecasting, in which planners extend the time horizons of the annual budgeting cycle. Few tackle externally oriented planning, in which factors such as market trends, the economy, demography, competition and the like drive the planning process. Fewer still are "strategically managed" so that the future context of the enterprise is the fundamental consideration of senior management.

However, most organizations, large or small, have some mix of short- and long-term goals which, even if not formalized, are implicit. In the absence of a formal strategic business plan, a strategic approach to planning for the new integrated systems can help identify these goals, the assumptions behind them, and issues which will be vital to success in the future.

TREND: The scope of systems planning is becoming broader
In addition to the deepening relationship between systems planning and business planning, systems planning is becoming broader in scope. Systems planning can no longer be equated to technology planning. The reason is simple.

In many ways the new systems cannot be viewed as consisting of technology alone since they include *social* and *environmental* components as well. The social component consists of the human and organizational aspects of the new work system, such as new jobs, responsibilities, procedures, workflow, communications patterns, career paths, policies and organizational structures. The environmental components of the system include the physical layout of the office, the lighting, furniture and configuration of special facilities such as computer rooms.

Figure 3.1 illustrates how a change in the technology will ripple through the rest of the work system and cause or require changes in its social and environmental components.

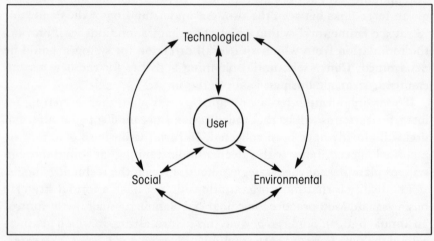

Figure 3.1   Three Components of an Integrated Office System

One of the central challenges of planning for integrated office systems is to formulate the social and environmental architectures which correspond to the overall needs of the enterprise and which will work together as part of a new work system.

When integrated systems implementation is contemplated, it can also be viewed as a catalyst for change — change that will ultimately impact on the people and their jobs, the procedures and policies that govern an efficient operation, and on the business goals of the organization itself.

This does not mean that planners will, or should, design individual jobs or workstations, but that the human and environmental implications of most personnel using an electronic workstation should be factored into the picture. Specifically, planners can formulate corporate *policies* regarding how the human and environmental issues should be approached within various individual departments.

TREND: Planning for computer, telecommunications and office technologies is converging
As the three technologies converge, the need for unified planning becomes more important. Often the first symptom of a problem due to sepa-

rate planning exercises is organizational confusion over who's in charge of what. The following scenario is typical. The DP manager has recently completed a long-range systems plan for traditional computer systems, including a plan to refine and extend the national data communications network. The manager of Administration, who is responsible for word processing, decides to lease some long distance lines to enable the construction of a national word-processing network. Several line managers decide to implement a local area network in their department to link personal computers together. And at the same time, the manager of Corporate Telecommunications is recommending the purchase of a digital PBX (private branch exchange) telephone switch, which will also enable communication of data between proposed display-telephone workstations.

To the DP manager, the whole thing looks like "data processing". To the rest, a comment like that hints of a power play by the Systems department. To the senior executive, the whole situation looks like trouble.

While this "organizational" or turf issue has been prominent, there are deeper underlying reasons why a unified approach to planning makes much sense. A unified approach is required to

- prevent massive duplication of effort;
- enable an overall strategy for technology which is rooted in business needs;
- free line managers and end-user groups to plan systems which are appropriate for them within the framework of global plans, policies and standards.

The aim is to give each member of the enterprise appropriate access to corporate systems resources, and to people and facilities outside their work group. So it is necessary to build a network strategy which can enable appropriate compatibility between computing resources throughout the organization.

Having said this, it is clear that there are, and will continue to be, aspects of planning for all three technologies which are best done independently. In particular, many traditional data-processing applications, designed to improve the efficient processing of structured information, and for which there are no foreseeable MIS applications, may best be handled somewhat separately.

However, the general trend remains. Information in computers of all sizes through the organization will constitute the corporate database. The telephone system will become part of the corporate communications network. Administrative or office technologies like word processors or intelligent photocopiers will provide input and output devices on the network. A unified approach to the formulation of general direction, corporate-wide requirements, policies and standards is increasingly necessary.

This growth of the domain of integrated office systems planning is illustrated in Figure 3.2.

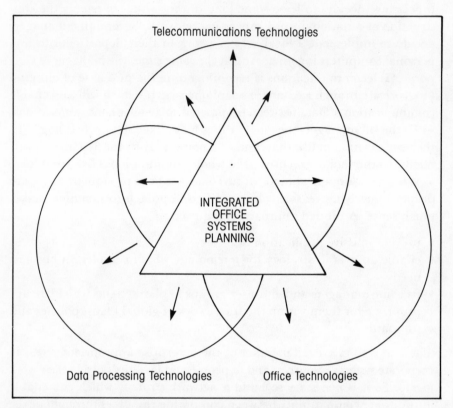

Figure 3.2 The Expansion of Integrated Office Systems Planning

TREND: The process of planning is becoming as important as the plan itself

An organization is in many ways a sea of forces through which a plan has to navigate. There are various people with different values, perspectives, interests and political or power objectives, each of whom has a stake in the plan. The planning *process* is one of achieving a common vision, or a collective perspective that fits the needs of the organization and is acceptable to the stakeholders. In this sense the planning process is as important as the product of planning — the integrated systems plan itself.

An example from a Fortune 500 corporation will help to highlight the importance of the process itself. Over the years this organization gained a reputation for using the latest and most sophisticated systems. The corporation's plan for integrated office systems was developed by the Information Planning department, in isolation. Sponsorship for its strategy had been obtained via separate sessions with each of the line organization vice presidents, and did not include their respective staff members responsible for systems implementation. In the end, months of creative, diligent work on the part of the Information Planning group, in researching, developing and producing the plan, slid slowly and painfully to its final resting place, gathering dust on a shelf. Why?

Without the collective input, support and involvement of line and staff representatives of groups such as Computer Systems, Organization and Methods, Human Resources, Administrative Services, Telecommunications, the Unions, Business Planning and senior executives from the vice presidents up to the Board of Directors, *the plan was doomed from the start*. Without the sponsorship and commitment of top management and without full coordination across departments within the organization, the planning effort cannot succeed.

It would be a mistake, for example, to allow a consulting company to draft an integrated systems plan independently. Plans must be developed by those who will be affected and by those who have responsibility for implementing them. A consultant may have an important role to play, but when all is said and done, it's your plan. It must be forged by and implemented by you and the key people in your organization. Because of this, there is a clear focus shift away from the plan itself and towards the people who should be involved in the process.

TREND: Bottom-up as well as top-down planning

Good traditional systems plans were always based on information provided by end-users, line managers and senior management. Nevertheless traditional systems plans were top-down plans, formulated by DP management for computer systems which were implemented by a central group. This situation was not necessarily due to the meglomaniacal tendencies of the "high priests of data processing", as some have argued.[1] Rather, it originated more in the nature of traditional DP systems, which were owned by a central authority, had little effect on end-users, and whose design and use required a high level of technical competence.

Chip technology is turning this situation on its head. The proliferation of independent computing gear, such as personal computers and word processors, initiated some fundamental changes in the ownership and control of technology as well as the nature of systems planning. For the first time, computer technology was being acquired directly by end-users, work groups and other organizational units on a mass scale. Also for the first time, large numbers of non-technical people in offices were taking initiatives to use computers on the job.

While the negative potential of the organization flying off in a myriad of directions is obvious, there are fundamentally positive aspects of this reversal which must be factored into the systems planning process. To begin, the diffusion of electronic workstations throughout the organization, and the transformation of the ways that people work and the organization does its business will only take place with the active involvement of the users and management at all levels. This desire for a role, a voice, some authority, or some control over the technology, contributes to a sense of responsibility on the part of users. Only when users accept such responsibility for their use of technology and feel that the new tools of office work truly belong to them can the huge potential of the technology be realized.

Not only is it *undesirable* for a central systems group to independently plan and implement the new technologies throughout the organization, in most medium or large organizations it is *simply not possible*. A central group with the resources to assess user requirements, plan, design, implement, evaluate, monitor, refine, extend and evolve electronic workstations throughout the organization, would be an organizational monstrosity.

For example, at the Stanford Research Institute International in Palo Alto, California, there are approximately 110 different disciplines, all with varying needs for integrated office systems. It would be almost impossible to set up something at the corporate level to serve everyone. So there are standards which govern the types of word processors and personal computers used by the employees. Beyond this, it is up to the users themselves to choose, implement and operate the systems in a manner which works for their respective departments.

It makes sense for the systems function to play a leadership role in formulating overall strategy, technical standards and many policies, along with the planning and implementation of corporate-wide computer resources such as networks, data-processing systems and databases which will be used by several departments. At the same time, the unique needs of various individuals, work groups and departments can be assessed and addressed by those directly involved, within the overall planning framework.

The result of this is that planning will continue to be top-down where overall plans are required. But planning is also becoming bottom-up where people throughout the organization will be involved in various aspects of planning what technology is best for them.

Consequently, the *role of the systems function* is changing. Rather than being the owner, planner, designer, implementor and controller of systems, the systems function is becoming a facilitator, educator, stimulus, and source of technical knowledge. It must be both a leader and participant in the process of co-producing systems plans with those who will use technology.

While system planning is becoming "bottom-up", it is also becoming even more "top-down" than in the past. The Systems department has a critical role to play, although that role is changing. But as technology becomes more important to the success of the enterprise, it is even more important that the entire senior management team takes responsibility for it. This is necessary to ensure that systems strategy meets corporate goals; that senior management "own" the strategy, enabling the resources required to implement it; and that the opportunities to directly support the senior management team with the new technology are fully exploited.

TREND: Implementation of integrated systems and planning for them go hand in hand

Data processing systems were implemented once planning was complete. A long-range systems plan was put in place, listing the applications to be developed. The design and development people then started to make their way through the list, producing systems which were delivered to the user departments.

The preceding scenario is really not feasible when it comes to integrated systems for a number of reasons. First, it is likely that "implementations" of multifunction workstations are taking place in your organization right now — multi-tasking personal computers, display telephones and even integrated office systems pilots.

Second, it is unlikely that any of the key players — be they senior management, systems people or user departments — will really understand what the new technology is all about, what the opportunities for improvement are, and how to plan for integrated technology without some actual experience using it. Consequently a planning process conducted in a vacuum will be too abstract. Likewise a plan formulated in the absence of real world experiences with the new technology will likely be off the mark. Worst of all, lacking evidence as to the benefits of integrated systems, derived from actual experiences in your organization, one may mistakenly conclude that there is little to be gained. Without implementations which point to potential corporate-wide opportunities and problems, there may well be no compelling motivation to plan at all.

A third factor is that in almost every organization, there is at least one person who is a natural innovator. These people are not necessarily in the DP department. In several cases we found it was the chief executive officer.

In others it has been an administrative assistant, an accountant, an engineer, or a marketing manager. If you have an office systems function in your organization you'll likely find one or more of these innovators there. That is, someone who understands the opportunities posed by the multifunction workstation and has a personal interest in seeing the organization go forward.

We have found that organizations move forward as these individuals gain credibility and authority. It is through successful implementations, where "the proof was in the pudding", that such individuals gain credibility and the environment for serious planning is fostered.

So, actual experience implementing systems provides motivation and knowledge for serious planning. The trend is therefore to undertake experimentation and the piloting of the new systems before the final plan is completed. We have found it best to initiate the two activities at the same time.

TREND: The information required for planning is changing
Traditional data-processing plans were preceded by some form of feasibility study, in which the structured information in the enterprise was described and charted and an assessment of the opportunities for displacing information-processing costs was made. When considering how to take advantage of the new converging technologies, it is probably even more important to base any plans on solid information. However, the information required is different than with traditional plans. First, there is less focus on the detailed description of data elements for structured information that is necessary for the detailed specification and design of traditional data-processing systems.

Rather, it is more important to define what types of data have corporate-wide implications and should therefore be subject to corporate-wide planning policies. Other types of data will be unique to various departments and should be left to those departments to rationalize.

Second, the *scope* of the information to be collected will be broader. Information is required on:

- The economic, social and political context surrounding the enterprise as it begins planning
- The strengths and weaknesses of the organization and key obstacles to meeting objectives
- The forecast of technology in general
- Where the opportunities for integrated systems lie within the organization
- What the climate for change is within the organization

- Where the priorities for entry pilots should be
- The implications of integrated systems for human resource issues and also for the work environment and physical plant

Such information can come from a variety of sources. Throughout this book we will show how information can drive the process of planning to effectively harness the new technologies.

Organizing to Plan

The office of the future will be very difficult to achieve with the organization of the past. Until now, new technologies have generally meant new managers, or even departments, if the organization was large enough. Telephones created communications departments. Electronic number-crunching produced the DP department. Photocopiers and other office technologies resulted in groups overseeing "administrative technologies" within administration departments.

The extension of these technologies and their integration is blurring organizational lines. Indeed, many organizations have become immobilized because of difficulty in sorting out the thorny problems regarding who should lead the new planning effort.

Inevitably office systems have an impact on the power relationships in the organization. When systems are introduced gradually into the communication and decisionmaking process of an organization, aspects of power become extremely important. Who will have a greater influence as a result of these new systems — the computer specialist, the administration manager, the corporate finance vice president, or the individual line manager?

The processing and planning capabilities of the new technology can impart authority to the division in charge of it. Because of the personal computer, more and more departments within organizations have control over much of the information relevant to their work. At the same time they require a communications network which goes beyond their departmental boundaries. So, for many people, control of the network will really be the major issue.

How can you organize for planning, given that resolution of such "organizational questions" takes time and experience? How can you prevent these issues of power from blocking the planning process? — a process which, ironically, is necessary to resolve the problem itself.

At the heart of the control problem is the need for senior management to be involved and to lead the process. A strategy must be devised to alter the management reward system to motivate managers to participate constructively, and in the interests of the organization as a whole.

The general trend is towards new ad hoc organizational forms called *coalitions* which can cross traditional functional lines. These coalitions can have mandates to join forces, resources and ideas to come to grips with the issues that are posed by these new systems. Accordingly, a new reward/motivation structure stems from the mandate of the coalition: to leave behind old notions and ways, clearing the path for fresh ideas, cooperation and coordinated effort in new directions.

IBM Canada provides us with an excellent working model of a coalition. Figure 3.3 illustrates the structure of this group, whereby all of the required participants have clearly defined roles and responsibilities. Full-time staff have been assigned to both the planning activities and to implementation, with complete user-department involvement. Each user department has a director whose responsibilities include cross-functional liaison on projects involving agreement on access to data resources, communications of planning objectives, strategies and implementation coordination.

The Project Office, which consists of full-time staff, reports to the highest decisionmaking body in the organization, the Operations Review Committee (comprised of the Chairman, President, and two senior vice presi-

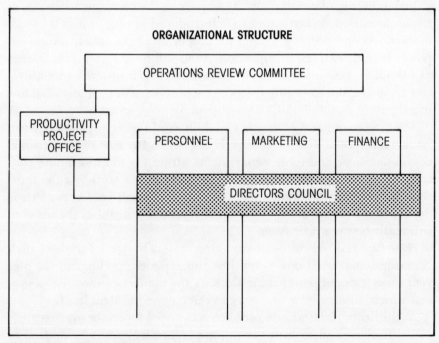

Figure 3.3 IBM Coalition Model

dents). This high-level reporting relationship ensures that conflicts among the user departments can be resolved without prolonged battles.

Top level management involvement and commitment is so crucial to the successful implementation of the plan that a recent study of 236 top-level executives representing a cross section of 195 U.S. industrial companies, has cited it most frequently as the reason for failure to achieve desired results.[2]

The involvement of the people responsible for implementing the plan is also key to building a successful process for planning. However, too often the office systems planning group is an organizational unit set apart from line and staff groups. In planning for these systems, the degree of involvement and participation across the organization, especially with the implementors, must be broadened.

There are numerous ways to put this structure in place. An ad hoc committee composed of various department members, or a formal steering committee, or an actual integrated office systems function are all possible options.

Steering committees tend to be high level groups appointed to coordinate and guide specific organizational activities through to their conclusion. Most often, the steering committee members represent a broad cross section of the organization in order to ensure that the interests of all divisions or departments are fairly represented. The steering committee most often oversees the work of another group, the task force.

In the late 1970s and early 1980s, the concept of the office technology task force began to be accepted. This group, when sanctioned by top management, can play an important role in planning. Typically the task force participates in collecting and analyzing information, drafting planning documents and making recommendations to a steering committee or other senior management body.

The size of the task force may vary, but usually the smaller the better. Typically, the task force includes someone from MIS or data processing, a financial manager to assess costs and benefits and ensure funding, a human resources or personnel manager to assess user impact, a telecommunications manager to consider network implications and an administrative manager familiar with workflow analysis, word processing, graphics and reproduction.

For example, the Frito-Lay Corporation implemented a task force in the early 1980s. The task force was responsible for both short and long-range planning for a number of office systems. The task force had two levels. The first was a committee called the Advanced Office Systems Group (AOSG) headed by a systems development manager. AOSG members included experts in voice, image and text processing systems. This group advised a larger one called the Office Automation Committee (OAC). This latter committee included representatives of the corporate data-processing staff, telecommunications managers, word processing managers, a records processing manager and other key groups.

AOSG had the responsibility for day-to-day consulting to various user departments, but they also undertook long-range planning. For example, they were responsible for selecting workstation products for all levels of personnel, which would be compatible from a data and communications viewpoint. Although total integration is a number of years away in Frito-Lay, the task force has helped ensure that this goal is indeed possible.

A task force can play a vital role in making appropriate use of the new technologies. As a multi-disciplinary group, it can focus on global issues, assess corporate needs and recommend appropriate solutions which will realize gains in productivity and overall organizational effectiveness. The task force can play a vital role in getting the entire planning process started.

Planning Process and Components

Because there are many components to a strategic plan for integrated office systems, many aspects to the planning process and several different forms an implementation can take, the entire process has been mapped out on the inside covers of this book. You may find it useful to refer to this roadmap occasionally as you read through the book.

The roadmap outlines:

- the corporate-wide information which drives the planning process;
- the main components of an integrated office systems plan;
- the various forms of implementations;
- the information which is collected within individual departments or functions of the organization; and
- the relationships among all of the above.

Having laid all this out we can move on to the first piece of the plan — the Strategic Framework.

A BUSINESS FOUNDATION FOR STRATEGY

2

The Strategic Framework

Strategic planning is often considered a simple process of setting goals, along with a strategy for reaching those goals. While this may be literally correct, it misses the essence of the concept.

"Strategic" is a term that evolved from military operations, referring to the operations or movements previous to battle. In its simplest sense, it means creating a plan not only to win some battles, but also to win the war. This approach to planning allows the strategist to see the choices to be made and the resources to be allocated in order to position the military units in question for further advances in the future.

Such a concept has obvious applications to non-military enterprises — such as strategic planning for systems. To date, however, many organizations remain somewhat myopic when formulating office systems strategies and plans. Plans for word processing and telephone systems are generally constructed with short-term objectives of cost displacement. Often the same is true for data processing and even management information systems. Many so-called strategies have been developed in a vacuum without adequate consideration of the broader business context and relevant issues. As a result their impact on the organization is often limited, or "tactical", rather than "strategic". Such plans not only miss opportunities, but also poorly position the organization to survive a period where technology is becoming critical to business success.

This poses a considerable challenge to senior management. The need is to ensure that technology plans are not driven by technology, or by shortsighted or restricted assessments of opportunities, but by an understanding of the business context currently facing the enterprise and how that context will change in the future.

Some kind of Strategic Framework is generally accepted as the starting point for an overall business strategy as well as the basis for most theoretical planning models. A present and future context is framed, which determines to a great extent the content of the strategies to be used.

However, too often in the day-to-day struggle, management loses sight of the framework and the strategic and becomes immersed in more operational issues. It is only during some important shift or new development, such as an economic recession, that the context is brought into question. It is a thesis of this book that the new converging technologies provide such a shift — a shift which requires re-evaluation of the context surrounding your organization.

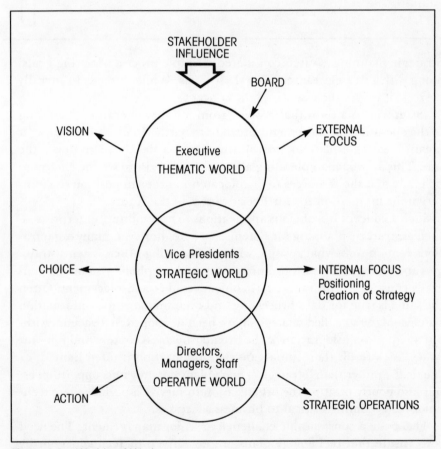

Figure 4.1   Worlds of Work

Within the organization itself there are several "worlds of work", as shown in Figure 4.1, with corresponding organizational functions at each level. At the executive level, the future "vision" of the organization is determined and its mission defined in relation to the current and future context it faces. This is the foundation of all strategy. At the senior management level, strategic directions are formulated, objectives for achieving strategy are developed, and the organization is positioned within its marketplace to realize those objectives. These objectives are communicated to the operative world, where they are implemented. Problems arise when all of management becomes immersed in the operative world.

So it is with planning to harness the new technologies. A fundamental objective of executives and senior management must be to think and plan "strategically", and ensure that office systems plans and overall strategic business plans are consistent.

If a strategic business planning process exists within your organization, you may have already assessed your business context and constructed much of the framework described in the remainder of this chapter. You may still find it valuable to review the material here to map our view of the contextual information which is desirable against that information which you have at hand.

If, however, your organization's business plan does not have an adequate assessment of the present and future context, it is probably useful to undertake the activities described in the rest of the chapter. The reader should note that the process described here is *not* a complete strategic business planning process. There is already a massive body of literature on this topic. Rather, we are suggesting a strategic approach to planning for office systems that

- uses elements of strategic business planning to establish the framework for office systems strategy, *and*
- calls for new sources of information and considerations *beyond* those required for business planning, to construct a strategy for integrated office systems.

A Strategic Framework for integrated systems should contain three components:

An **environmental scan** of the external trends and events whether political, societal or economic, which may have an impact on the organization's existing and future mission. By monitoring these trends and events, the enterprise will gain a picture of the external environment in which it will exist within the planning horizon. This scanning activity should surface *critical issues* which can be tracked further, so that appropriate action can be taken.

A competitive or comparative analysis of the business or public sector agency. This internal **organizational assessment** provides a picture of the organization's position relative to the larger industrial or public sphere.

This permits an evaluation of the organization's strengths and weaknesses as well as the obstacles which must be overcome in order to perform effectively in the marketplace.

A **forecast of** of how traditional **technologies** will evolve to form integrated office systems, the potential these systems offer for the enterprise generally, and the problems others have encountered in implementing and planning for effective utilization and overall benefit.

In combination, these three analyses will provide a working model, or picture, of the future environment, the climate for business and operations, and the potential opportunities which technology can provide. The majority of this information is external to the enterprise and helps construct an "outside-in" view of the current state of affairs, from which it is possible to determine a vision of *"what should be"*. This can result in a revised statement of mission and overall organizational objectives, as well as a general projection of how the new technology can help achieve those objectives.

Still working at a global level, the next challenge is to determine the factors which will ensure successful attainment of this mission and its inherent goals. Such *"critical success factors"* will form a bridge to strategy — the formulation of an overall direction, or the answer to the question of *"how* can we realize our new objectives?"* The relationship of the information required for strategic business planning versus strategic planning for integrated office systems is depicted in Figure 4.2. Elements of this diagram will be explained as we go along.

Environmental Scan

A scan of the external environment and its implications for the organization is a first step in the process of building a Strategic Framework. This is a scan of the external environment and an evaluation of the economic, political, social and other issues which will have an impact on the organization, its objectives and its plans to use technology. (For possible environmental factors see Figure 4.3.)

To take an example from the manufacturing sector, let's look at a company whose business is the brewing, bottling and distribution of beer. The environment would be scanned for information relating to the impact of an increasing number of older people in society (since beer drinkers tend to be young, between the ages of nineteen and thirty-two), public opinion towards such social issues as drinking and driving, statistics on alcoholism and rising per capita consumption, and government regula-

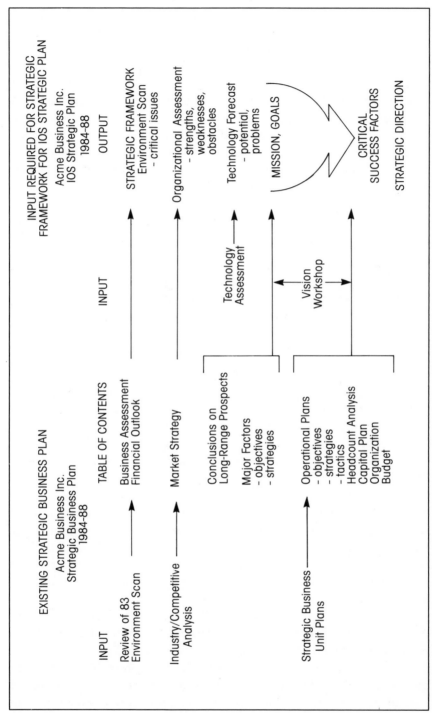

Figure 4.2 Information Required for Business versus Systems Planning

tions on pricing, taxation and import quota relaxation. Such information could have implications for the general future of the business, expansion plans and, possibly, plans to pursue new objectives or even markets.

Another interesting trend might be a noted preference for cans or uniquely shaped and colored bottles — indicating that manufacturing technology must be flexible. Changing preferences and buying trends also indicate a need for instant sales feedback from distribution outlets and for the organization to respond quickly to change. These issues will have relevance to the future business of this organization. They must be *tracked* in order to determine anticipated volume, consumer acceptance, and profitability. For it is the cumulative effect of these trends that could determine the future viability of the business.

Changes in attitudes and/or behavior of general public and/or opinion leaders

Shifts in activities of stakeholder groups such as stockholders, lenders, employees, customers, competitors, suppliers, special interest groups

Changes in fiscal/monetary policy, price indices, currency fluctuations

Shifts in programs, decisions, enforcement procedures of regulatory agencies

Legislative initiatives at all levels of government deliberations—from international to local levels

Outcome of significant litigation and/or court rulings

New theories and/or proposals from academic and research groups relative to the organization's scope of endeavor

Scientific and technological innovations

Figure 4.3 Possible Environmental Factors

Once the structure for ongoing scanning, monitoring and evaluation is set in place, it is a matter of continually scanning the various sources of this information to update and take a reading at planning time. This scan will continually surface critical issues which may impact on the organization, and which may require the discussion and resolution by key management.

Tracking these critical issues can allow for a more proactive or anticipatory, approach to management, rather than waiting for these issues to become problems. These issues have an important role in defining the framework for the plan, as they may become real obstacles to the strategic direction that will also be chosen. Conversely, they may work for the organization, if they are identified early, and managed in a fruitful, constructive way.

Business/Organization Assessment

Information about the external environment and the critical issues which require ongoing tracking and attention, provides the planner with knowledge of the larger world in which the organization must operate. The next stage in determining the framework, or future context of the organization, is that of assessing the business or industry environment, the competitive situation (including threats and opportunities), and competitive strategies. In public sector organizations, a comparative analysis will serve a similar purpose.

Having done these analyses, an evaluation can be made of how suitable various internal business strategies are in meeting the emerging business challenges. This analysis will provide the information necessary to review the organization's major strengths, weaknesses and obstacles to achieving success and dominance in the marketplace, or in out-maneuvering the competition. This will also position your organization to map the emerging opportunities presented by new technology against your assessment of the enterprise's strengths and weaknesses.

We recommend that a complete assessment should include three perspectives: 1) your industry's, 2) your competition's and 3) your own organization's. Let's consider each in turn.

1. Your Industry
The industry or total environment within which your organization provides products or services and competes is of course an essential part of the context within which competitive strategy must be formulated.

A scan of an industry would involve an assessment of the life-cycle of products/services, their relevance to market need and broader societal expectations within a horizon of five to ten years. As well as product/service line, other areas such as industry-wide technical developments, labor relations, manufacturing innovations, distribution and marketing trends and target markets need to be assessed. An understanding of these factors and industry trends will contribute to defining the overall opportunities and threats posed to your business/organization over the long term. Establishing an *industry viewpoint* will provide an important perspective within which both the competition and your own business/organization can be comparatively evaluated, and strategy formulated.

2. Your Competition
There is a wealth of material on competitive evaluation. For example, in *Competitive Strategy: Techniques for Analyzing Industries and Compe-*

titors Michael Porter writes that competitive analysis should include an assessment of competitors'

- **Future goals**. This enables predictions as to competitor's future behavior in response to changes in the environment.
- **Current Strategy**, including an assessment of operating policies and tactics in the market, as well as an evaluation of the competition's use of technology, especially as a strategic weapon.
- **Assumptions**, about its own situation, such as being a low-cost producer, at the top of the market-share ladder or a socially conscious firm.
- **Capabilities**, including its strengths — especially its weaknesses and ability to make strategic changes in a changing environment.

As technology becomes a decisive weapon in competitiveness, it is important to have a clear assessment of the current status of the competition. Such understanding enhances your ability to identify opportunities for improvement or strategic advantage.

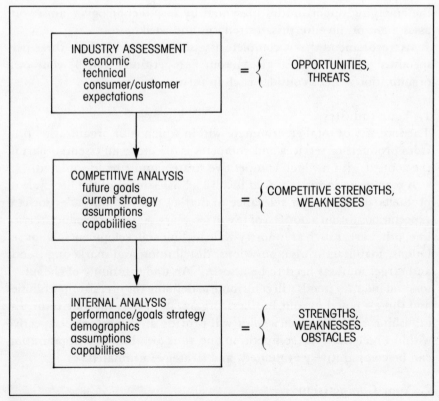

Figure 4.4   Business/Organizational Assessment

3. Your Own Company

The competitive analysis will yield a view of specific major competitor strategies, strengths, weaknesses and obstacles. This information can be critical input to the formulation of your own strategies and goals. However, before they can be clearly and confidently defined, a similar analysis of internal factors must be made. This will probably require the collection of information within the organization. Useful information can be obtained from structured interviews of selected managers and other personnel, secondary source information from within the enterprise, and through other sources such as questionnaires and group discussions.

When complete, the business/organization assessment should provide the knowledge needed to specify the organization's overall strengths, weaknesses and the opportunities and obstacles to achieving objectives. This is depicted in Figure 4.4.

An example of an organization assessment conducted in a large professional association may be helpful here. This was the first time this process had been undertaken, and the fact that it was precipitated by a desire to investigate and plan for the introduction of integrated office systems illustrates how their introduction can often provide the catalyst needed to begin strategic planning. The organization decided it had the following:

1. Strengths

- Highly visible political profile, influencing policy and legislation
- Largest association of its kind in the country
- Large capital assets which can be leveraged for funding purposes
- In-house technology base from which to migrate into integrated office systems.

2. Weaknesses

- Crisis-driven — often responding to actions of government on a daily basis
- One-year planning horizon, compounded by organizational structure requiring yearly elections
- Development and communication of long-term objectives in order to provide a better focus of time and energy needed.

3. Obstacles

- Lack of time — conflicting demands, difficulty in scheduling meetings, reactive environment

- Poor communications/information — lack of timely communication, causing dissension, lack of coordinated view of events, too much paper to be meaningfully assimilated by staff
- Funding — declining numbers, rising costs
- Overloaded data processing system — obsolete hardware, at capacity, with two-year applications backlog
- Work environment — building wiring overloaded, outmoded phone system
- Attitudes — lack of awareness of future potential of new systems, resistance to change, fear of technology.

Technology Forecast

In addition to the environmental scan and the business assessment just described, it is necessary to develop a forecast of the new technology. This will provide your management team with a common view of where the technology is headed; what general capabilities are evolving; what opportunities for improving productivity and organizational performance will present themselves; and what the main problems in taking advantage of these opportunities are.

This book will not provide you with the "technology forecast" itself, other than to indicate some general trends in technology. However a few comments are in order regarding what should be included in the forecast, what the planner should be trying to achieve in researching the wealth of information from vendors, in the media, from consultants, and in technology-scanning reports.

Forecasting technology requires some homework, some visits to other organizations, and some discussion among the appropriate persons in your enterprise. One way of handling this technological jungle is to start with the "trigon", or triangle of converging technologies and to examine how the vendors from all three corners are migrating towards the center — integrated office systems. Particular attention should be paid to the strategies of those vendors already represented in the organization, whether in the form of mainframe computers or word processors.

There are additional issues of forecasting you may want to investigate. How well are these technologies being applied generally; and, specifically, what is the competition doing in terms of implementation and planning? Where do the real opportunities lie? What does the literature say about success or failure in implementations to date, and what are the predictions for the next period? Where do the major problems and pitfalls lie, and what has been done to overcome these obstacles to successful use of technology?

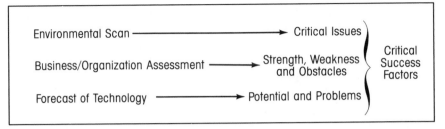

Figure 4.5   Building the Strategic Framework

Building the Framework

As illustrated in figure 4.5, this work must be consolidated in a Strategic Framework, upon which an integrated systems strategy can be built. To summarize, you will have collected and analyzed:

- External information at the societal, political and economic level, and the resultant critical issues;
- An assessment of the organization (within its industrial or public sector context), outlining its strengths, weaknesses and key obstacles to achieving success; and
- The forecast of how technology may impact on the organization's performance, along with an assessment of the main problems posed by technological change.

This should provide you with the information necessary to define the future context of the organization. It should also provide insights into how the objectives, goals, and even mission of your enterprise may change in the light of this evolving framework.

In general, it is important that discussions of these issues involve the right people in your organization. One way of facilitating such discussion is to have a Vision Workshop or planning workshop. A central objective of such a discussion should be to extract factors for the success of the organization over the planning horizon — the critical success factors. As was the case with the topic of strategic planning as a whole, there is a wealth of literature on the topic of critical success factors, or "CSFs" as they are sometimes called. The difference here is that for the first time the strategic importance of the new technology is being factored into the formulation of such success factors.

Much of the discussion about the information this process has generated will be rather informal. This Vision Workshop may be the first in a series of *more formal* workshops which will take place throughout the planning process. The intent of this first session is to shape the future context of the organization. Both the analyses and presented facts combine to support a discussion of where the organization should be heading, and what it will be when it gets there.

One organization which we helped through this process was able to expand its mission beyond the business they thought they were in. This non-profit organization was in the business of developing standards for electronic products, and then certifying those products as meeting a given standard. Through the process of strategic planning for integrated systems they were able to envision the day when they would be in the "information provider" business. That is, they saw a general opportunity to automate the process of designing standards and certifying products through integrated technologies. The environmental scan revealed that the requirements of their business were changing and they were coming under pressure to:

- Respond better to public information demands
- Provide higher quality information products
- Remain competitive
- Facilitate new and expanded services associated with those information products.

One of the critical success factors of this organization was technology itself. The massive explosion of technology, the anticipated pervasiveness of terminals in most of this organization's consumer locations, and the opportunities afforded by online access to information, led to the conclusion that the business could change. It was decided to shift the business focus from a two-year development process of standards to instant retrieval of standards and certification information.

Therefore, one of their major success factors was the introduction of new technology and systems to support online access to and retrieval of information.

Another factor that would be critical to success was to position the organization within the marketplace as a leading-edge, modern organization — one whose name would be identified with a valuable, available, accurate source of information.

A third was to establish the necessary skill base within the organization's management team. New expertise was required to change strategy towards technology-oriented products and services.

The organization is a good example of how an assessment of the business context, including trends in new technology, can lead to plans to change the nature of the business. It is unlikely that a traditional systems planning process would have led to similar conclusions.

A small organization will have essentially the same structure for this section of the plan, but on a correspondingly smaller scale. Of necessity, the resources required to pull this information together are scarcer. As a result, there may be a temptation to skip this part of the planning process. However, doing so will compromise the crucial linkage which ties the introduction of technology, its evolution, and the planning for capital expenditures on technology to the overall mission and goals to be achieved by the organization.

At one time, Trigon Systems Group Inc. was a small organization of about twenty people, primarily professional consultants. In building our strategic plan for integrated systems, we held management planning sessions where we collectively discussed the external environment (social, political, economic), and recorded the critical issues we saw arising from our joint assessment. We used the technology in the meeting room to capture our thoughts and used this information to produce a systems plan and also for future reference. Through the process of re-examining our plans for technology we concluded that our business was changing. State-of-the-art technology, we decided, was not only necessary for Trigon to be a high performance organization and to "practice what we preach"; but would enable us to provide new services and educational products and stay competitive in a changing world.

Large or small, it is doubtful that you can afford to ignore the external environment in shaping your organization and its use of technology. The price of indifference may mean failure to meet the challenges posed by other economic, market and societal shifts, so bringing into question success and survival in the information age.

So it is on the basis of a vision of what the organization is to be and the goals required to get there, along with the critical success factors, that the strategic direction can be set. These factors will also provide the basis for a successful implementation of systems.

The Strategic Direction

Assessing Global Opportunities

To quote from the strategic plan for integrated systems of one of our clients:

> Without a true understanding of the real world of the office — its mission, tasks, and the way it functions — the wrong things will be automated, the wrong services offered and the wrong technology will be implemented.

Once the external context for systems has been defined, it is necessary to turn your attention towards corporate-wide, or "global" opportunities for using the new technology to improve productivity and achieve other objectives. This requires an internal corporate-wide investigation which we refer to as an "Opportunity Analysis".

Too often, an enterprise suffers from conflict or indecision because it has little objective information regarding its *current* state of affairs. This information must be well in hand before new directions can be forged, since it often makes the difference between strategy that will work and that which will leave you simply groping in the darkness of misinformation.

An accurate picture of the current state of the organization will:

- provide input to help determine where the major opportunities for integrated systems lie;
- provide concrete facts so that each of the planning participants can discuss issues from a common base of knowledge;
- provide useful direction as to the priority areas for implementation of a pilot system or an entry project;
- raise awareness across the organization of the opportunities the technology can present (what is possible), and provide a chance to discuss obstacles and problems management currently faces, from a perspective of objectivity.

Such an Opportunity Analysis can also include an assessment of human resources, providing information on demography, management depth, knowledge of technology, attitudes towards change, motivation and the climate regarding the introduction of the technology and possible organizational change.

In any case, the first objective of this assessment is to collect the information required to *identify* in sufficient detail *opportunities* for improving administrative support, information management, communications, decision support and other services within the organization. The goal will be not only to find out what managers and other personnel *think* is needed, but also to evaluate *actual* requirements, perhaps in less obvious targets such as time-use, communications patterns, decision support, and other critical processes.

These opportunities can be grouped together as appropriate and analyzed with respect to their potential for a) cost reduction, b) cost avoidance, and c) improvements in the effectiveness of the organization and its personnel.

To begin, here are some techniques of acquiring the required information:

1. Collection of Secondary Source Material
Helpful material can be obtained from sources such as organizational charts, statements of objectives, reports from previous studies, systems plans, demographic data, communication bills and floor plans. This information often contributes to an understanding of the information pathways within the organization and the characteristics of that information.

2. Technology Scan
Current computer, office, telephone and other technologies within the organization should be inventoried, at a level of detail sufficient to determine what components of the currently installed base of technology can form part of the new office systems plans.

3. Interviews of Key Personnel
These interviews raise questions regarding such issues as:

• The goals and objectives for the next fiscal year of an organizational unit.
• The information required for decisionmaking, the sources of this information, and the form in which the information is received.
• Overall communications patterns within the corporation.

Having collected this information, you have begun to construct a Strategic Direction. But you are still a long way off from implementing a system.

Three examples have been chosen to illustrate the range and potential impact these opportunities can have on an organization and *its mission*. In each case the *statement* of *global opportunities* was taken from the executive summary of a strategic plan for integrated systems.

Federal Government Department: To use integrated office systems to help hold the line on expenses without reducing the quality of service provided by the Department, and as human resources are more effectively utilized over time, to provide not only a leaner, but a better (more responsive, useful, relevant) service to the public, and in doing so to better realize the overall mission and goals of the Department.

Financial Institution: The productivity of the staff has historically not been given a lot of attention. However, the existence of ceilings on assets raises questions regarding the advisability of continuing such an approach. The organization cannot continue to be profitable by simply continuing to put assets on the books. It is now more important to be more selective about what services are offered, the process by which they are offered, and also to ensure that the organization has a high internal efficiency, and a marketing staff that spends its time productively and effectively.

Standards Organization: There are many opportunities to build a firm foundation within the organization from which to expand our world to a more externally-driven organization, and to enable a more proactive and responsive approach to the development of our products and services. This foundation will be built by improving the efficiency and effectiveness of our people; the management of our information and the actual process of producing our products. There are many ways in which the careful application of new information and communication technologies can provide time savings and other benefits which can be reinvested and applied to expand its horizons. Further, the organization's world can then be expanded to provide access to products and services via communications networks which connect branches, agencies, committees and members — the whole community of internal users. Over time that network can be extended to provide online access to information products and services to its consumers.

In the examples illustrated, the range and degree of impact of opportunities are quite different. The range extends from enabling the organization to essentially hold the line while providing better existing services to changing the nature of the products and services offered.

Conceptual Framework for Assessing Internal Opportunities

As pointed out first by Tapscott in *Office Automation: a User-Driven Method*, there are a number of different conceptual approaches regarding where the main opportunities for integrated office systems lie. Each approach is quite different, with different advocates in the industry and with different conclusions regarding where to focus your efforts in assessing requirements and evaluating systems. It is important that these opportunities are understood at the corporate level so that appropriate corporate methods may be employed throughout the planning process. These approaches are:

- **Organizational Communications Approaches**. These approaches view the organization as a communication system. The objective of office systems, for those holding this view, is to improve communications resulting in time savings, increased collaboration, better access to other personnel, improved organizational communications, and more control over communications in general.
- **Information Resource Management Approaches**. These approaches go beyond traditional MIS approaches to view office systems as enabling effective management of the information resource. Like money, people and materials, information should be treated as a resource that must be managed. The new technology can get the right information to the right people at the right time in a cost-effective manner.
- **Decision Support Approaches**. These approaches situate office system planning in the context of supporting the judgment of managers and other decisionmakers in their unstructured or semi-structured activities. From this framework, the objective of office systems requirements analysis and evaluation is to identify opportunities for and measure the impact of office systems on the performance of decision-making activities, especially those which involve management analysis of numbers.
- **Functional Approaches**. These emphasize the impact of office systems on the underlying functions which the office was created to fulfill. To functional practitioners, other approaches mistakenly confuse the ends (functions) that the office is realizing with the means (for example, communications) used to achieve them. To improve office functions, senior management should focus on the new technology to improve office procedures.
- **Quality of Work Life Approaches**. QWL approaches emphasize the impact of office systems on the nature of work, the motivation of the worker and the design of jobs and organizations. QWL utilizes an intervention strategy called "sociotechnical systems analysis and design." The objective of those taking this approach is to "jointly optimize" the social and technical aspects of a given work system[1].

It is important, as part of the formulation of a Strategic Framework and a Strategic Direction for integrated office systems, that some form of conceptual framework to office systems be formulated. It may be one of the above, a combination of the above or a new approach.

Opportunity Areas

In virtually all of the opportunity analyses we have conducted, there has been no difficulty in finding an abundance of opportunities for improvement. In many cases, it is the first time that the organization has taken a good look at where improvements might be made, and has actually solicited the opinion and involvment of all senior management in this process of self-examination.

Opportunities for improvement will depend to a great extent on

- the individual characteristics of the enterprise (size, geographic dispersion, degree of systems utilization at this point, receptivity to change), and
- the degree to which senior management is willing to take a hard look at improving efficiency, effectiveness and performance within their own functional groups and the organization as a whole.

However, in conducting corporate-wide studies like this since the mid-1970s, we have found that most opportunities can be grouped into opportunity areas corresponding to the five conceptual approaches. In fact it is important to group them into such categories and not take a "shotgun approach" towards assessing opportunities. Only then will you have a clear idea of the types of opportunities you are chosing as your focus — and the implications of that choice.

1. Improved Communications

Given geographical dispersion, or intense internal communications within an organization, the importance of timely, concise, cost-effective communications cannot be underestimated. There are often considerable opportunities to reduce the number and associated costs of internal memoranda through electronic messaging and/or document transfer. In addition, there are opportunities to reduce the extent to which employees engage in "telephone tag" and the amount of time spent taking messages on incomplete calls.

Another important "communications" opportunity is *mail-logging* or *correspondence management*. Particularly in the public sector there is a requirement to track incoming correspondence — its source, request, dates for completion, delegation to, and follow-up. In one such organization we found senior secretaries spending two hours a day in logging, following up and monitoring the progress of internal memoranda. Electronic messaging can change this entire activity, since such tracking can be done through electronic tickler and follow-up systems, integrated with the messaging function. Not only is secretarial time saved, but often management will also spend less time searching for status information and through paper-based correspondence files.

Meetings and meeting management is often another high leverage opportunity to improve organizational communications. In many organizations, face-to-face meetings, both planned and unplanned, account for the majority of management time. Too frequently the results of these meetings do not justify the hours spent.

Many typical problems in this area have more to do with meeting management and protocol than systems-related opportunities. However, we have found that by marrying the technology and procedural change, it is possible to achieve better meetings. Agendas can be distributed via messaging well in advance, to enable adequate preparation and resolution of agenda items. Key items can be discussed with concrete results through online access to information during a meeting. Information can be projected directly from the system onto large screens, ensuring up-to-date data for decisionmaking and a reduction in slide preparation costs. Much telephone and written communication is usually required to coordinate time, location, duration, agendas, and other details that ensure a meeting is efficiently held. Scheduling tools can provide opportunities to improve the speed with which these meetings can be organized and coordinated, ensuring accurate communication of meeting variables and details.

Opportunities may exist to reduce the travel and time costs lost of traveling long distances to meetings, through a variety of teleconferencing systems. These opportunities must be carefully quantified because the initial investment in equipment and facilities can be high. Usually, a pilot or trial conference is held in order to compare the experience, cost and results of teleconferences versus traditional face-to-face meetings.

A review of current *telephone systems performance* and requirements may suggest opportunities to add additional telephone capabilities and provide better and more cost-effective central switching for both voice and data. Often, there is a good cost-displacement argument for replacing such systems, particularly if telecommunications costs can be reduced. With the variety of integrated voice/data terminals on the market today, the cost of having a handset and a terminal on the desk can be combined into one device and cost. New functionality and features for voice communications can provide time savings as well. For instance, some of the PBX manufacturers have provided voice messaging with their switch. For organizations with a great deal of external communications (from suppliers, customers, or the public), voice messaging can provide significant opportunities to reduce telephone tag, improve customer relations, and increase responsiveness.

2. Improved Information Management

The opportunities to improve both access to and management of information resources, be they paper or electronic, are often striking. Improved access to corporate information really has little to do with receiving greater quantity, but rather with more selective, timely access, with greater flexibility in format and media. This need reflects a certain frustration with the "MIS Era" where the name of the game was to provide more quantity in the form of large printouts with structured formats. Variations were accommodated through producing yet another report.

Opportunities for improved management of paper-based records include reducing the amount of space devoted to cabinets full of files that have not been purged, culled or archived for some period of time and are not subject to good records management policy and practices. Further, a recapture of the time and effort required to maintain and gain access to records which are not well-organized can present a significant opportunity across all staff levels. In one client organization, this opportunity represented a file space saving of 50 percent. IBM Canada consolidated records from forty-eight file cabinets into a mere six which supported the correspondence requirements of the entire headquarters. Only one copy was retained of each piece of correspondence, with central access of two to five minutes guaranteed to users.

Access to external or public information is often found to be a high priority opportunity. Because of changes to our overall economic structure, changes in the competitive balance among organizations now faced with a world marketplace, and the increasing demand for government and political information, this type of information may become crucial to many levels of management.

3. Improved Decision Support

Once access to electronically stored information is provided, decision support tools can be used to improve the overall assessment of risk, to perform "what-ifs", to construct budgets and analyze variances and many other similar analyses. For example, if budget creation and monitoring is being done manually, there may be opportunities to save time and increase flexibility to change or modify individual and composite pictures.

This information may be shown graphically in order to better indicate trends, past variance and comparative pictures. Such benefits tend to be qualitative rather than quantitative.

An Information Center, where users write decision support programs with the assistance of trained systems professionals and fourth-generation programming language tools, may provide significant opportunities to expedite applications development. These benefits can be quantified in terms of the cost-displacement opportunities of reducing the time, effort and cost of software development.

4. Process, Procedure Redesign and Streamlining

The process by which office products (such as reports, budgets, presentations, board submissions, position papers and planning documents) are created and produced is often in critical need of scrutiny and change. Improvements to identified product processes could include reducing the amount of time from trigger event to final output, streamlining of activities, reduced cost of production and increased quality of end-product, accuracy and ability to match product relevance to need. We found it was costing one organization approximately $11,000 in administrative costs to produce a thirteen-page submission for board approval of capital acquisitions. Hundreds of these were created each year and timing was crucial. That is, if a presentation date was missed, it was removed from the board meeting docket until next year.

Organizations where process analysis has been undertaken have seen cost reductions ranging from 45 to 85 percent. Typically, the emphasis has been on the production of the final product, rather than in planning, designing and coordinating or managing the process.

Electronic messaging substitutes for the creation, typing, photocopying, distribution, and filing of internal memoranda. Along with other improvements, such as improved access to and management of information resources, this frees secretarial time for delegation by management. Delegation opportunities can be identified through a discussion of process improvements, through a discussion of how management spend their time, and in looking at the items that are on the proverbial "to do" list.

Tools which can support improvements in administrative support include text editing or word processing for use by management, professionals and secretarial staff; also, time and activity management tools such as project management, meeting scheduling, ticklers, diaries and electronic to-do lists.

We have seen a general shift towards self-management of one's job and time. With these tools, there is greater opportunity for taking control of such things as reporting on the status of outstanding items or projects. If the system can manage the "status", then the professionals and management can concentrate on devising strategy and planning activities.

Cost savings can be realized as well since there will be less need for hiring temporary staff for peak periods, or overtime salary for permanent staff. Further savings will result from replacing obsolete administrative technology such as typewriters or convenience copiers with combination laser/copier technology.

5. Quality of Working Life

One of our clients assessed the overall opportunities for improvement with the express objective of improving the quality of working life of management and professional staff. For years, this organization had held the line on increasing staff, and everyone had absorbed an ever-increasing workload, without complaint. Senior management felt that the time was coming where a dissatisfaction with the large workload, the infringement on personal time and stress that this continuing situation was creating, would become a major obstacle to their continuing high performance. In fact, they feared the loss of valuable, highly trained people to competitors who could offer a more normal balance of work and home-life, along with the normal salary enticements.

The opportunities for improvement were then evaluated in terms of freeing up time to enable staff members to return to a normal workload level, to enable them to spend more time in market research, analysis and strategy, rather than in process and production activities.

Through the various implementations where we have been involved, we have noted that people are freed up from the redundant activities, the fruitless searching for information that is not accessible or indexed and the frustrating aspects of trying to reach people in order to communicate. Once this has been accomplished, they can concentrate on doing the activities that are commensurate with their salary and expertise. Once this happens, they become more satisfied with their efforts, feel a greater sense of accomplishment and self-worth — and overall quality in the job.

There are many other areas for improvement that we could use to illustrate what is required at this juncture in the plan, as the list is endless. However, the concept and ideas should be well made at this point. The statement of internal opportunities will help give everyone in the organization an initial perspective on the direction the technology should take in improving the overall internal efficiency and effectiveness of the organization.

Most of the benefits discussed above involve cost reduction and avoidance, the saving of time, improvement of decisionmaking and the general management and functioning of the enterprise. To complete the picture you will have to translate the benefits into tangible strategic opportunities. This involves the development of a *global cost-benefit forecast*, a *reinvestment model* for the saved time and the integration of the *Strategic Framework* into the picture. These topics are discussed next.

Global Cost-Benefit: A Forecast

Many a business case for an integrated system pilot has been met with the glazed eyes or outright hostility of senior management. Performing a cost-benefit analysis for systems whose impacts are difficult to predict, difficult to measure and downright complex has clearly been a challenge. Many systems which could have had a profoundly positive impact on the organization never got off the ground because of their architects' inability to cost-justify them. On the other hand, over-zealous user groups may conduct cost-justifications which are superficial and misleading simply to generate support for a decision they have already made.

You should also note that at this point it is not possible to conduct what is known as a "feasibility analysis" in systems planning. The information available from your internal opportunity analysis does not have sufficient detail to allow evaluation of the feasibility or the costs-benefits of proceeding with a system implementation. To examine the feasibility of a particular system implementation, such detailed data must be collected for a given department or work group.

It is, however, possible to evaluate the anticipated costs and benefits *at a global level*. The objective is not to finely assess the return on investment or feasibility. It takes a great deal more time to gather the kind of objective data necessary to do such an evaluation. Until a general feeling for direction and potential is established, it is better to present an esti-

		1984-85	1985-86	1986-87
1.	Finance & Admin (515)	30	75	320
2.	Corporate Planning (57)		6	20
3.	Executive (70)		2	5
4.	Regional Director (355)		22	100
5.	Group A (741)	20	35	30
6.	Group B (2241)		20	225
7.	Group C (2455)		10	50
8.	Group D (1069)		10	50
9.	Group E (1062)		20	200
		50	200	1000

Figure 5.1   Number of Terminals Installed by Group and Year

mate of the global impacts to decisionmakers within the organization as the basis upon which further work will be authorized. At that time more complete feasibility assessments can be made.

One of the first exercises in assessing global costs and benefits is to prepare a forecast of anticipated systems and workstation growth over each year within the planning horizon, by functional area. The table in Figure 5.1 shows one possible scenario for a three-year timeframe. Of particular note is year one, which indicates two pilot implementations, with gradual extension to other groups in years two and three. The number of people in each functional group is indicated in brackets beside the name.

The Cost Forecast

Assumptions made during the process of arriving at a forecast of the anticipated costs of implementing systems should be made clear before yearly cost projections are formulated. Here are some examples of these assumptions from the integrated systems plan of one of our clients:

- Based on the assessment of opportunities, and desired functionality to be presented to the end-user, on a projection of the declining costs of technology and estimates from a variety of vendors and consultants, an estimated per user cost of approximately $5,000 per workstation is assumed for the last planning year.
- The $5,000 estimate includes all hardware (workstations, peripheral devices, special wiring, storage, telecommunications devices such as modems and local area network attachment units and video conferencing devices), software (all office software, excluding specialized applications software), maintenance and installation costs.
- The cost can be considered "expense" — either a lease or discounted capitalization on a three-year payback.
- Excluded from these figures are time lost to training and education, incremental costs for data communications, and specialized applications software development.

The table in Figure 5.2 shows the breakdown of the anticipated systems costs by line item.

Additional cost estimates should be shown for:

- **Implementation**: staff salaries and benefits, consulting costs, outside courses and conferences, acquisition of training materials, and manuals.
- **Furniture**: New workstations, additional furniture such as printer tables, addition of runoffs, chairs and acoustic covers for printers.
- **Lighting**: Modifications to existing fluorescent lighting such as antiglare screens or panels, ambient or task lighting.

CAPITAL COSTS		
1.	Workstation (10/cluster)	$2,000
2.	Cluster controller (micro, disk storage, printer)	$30,000
3.	Local area network (for voice, data, co-ax, video)	$1,000/workstation
4.	Printers (2/cluster)	$5,000
5.	Mini computer with 100-300 terminals per mini • disk • printers • optional reader	$2,000/terminal
6.	Communications capital — video	$15,000
ONGOING EXPENSES		
7.	Communications — ongoing maintenance — ongoing software maintenance	10%/year of capital costs 10%/year of initial software
8.	Staff & materials costs for ongoing operations	$500/terminal

Figure 5.2 Estimated Systems Costs

The Benefits Forecast

Integrated office systems can substantially improve both the efficiency and effectiveness of an organization. Some definitions of terms are required in order to appreciate the levels of benefits and the improvements that can be effected. If an office is viewed as an organizational entity which takes "inputs" from support and supply groups and processes them into "outputs" to be consumed by customers, users or clients, then the following improvements are possible.

Reduced Inputs (hard dollar savings or avoidance)
Assessments of the inputs into the office such as costs of labor, materials or supplies, can be quantified, and cost savings can be derived by reducing those inputs that are unnecessary or not seen to be "least-cost" solutions. Such improvements can impact the cost side of the bottom line.

Internal Efficiency (soft dollar savings)
These are improvements *internal* to the office which don't necessarily affect either the "inputs" or "outputs". Integrated office systems can save people time in activities such as typing, looking for information, telephoning, filing. In some cases they can also avoid work altogether.

Effectiveness
Improvements can be made not just in the quantity of outputs or products of office work but also in their *quality*. For example, consider improved service to customers, better reports and presentations. Such improvements can impact the revenue side of the bottom line.

Productivity
This concept is used synonymously with "organizational performance" to
refer to the overall ratio between input and output in the office. This
ratio can be improved in terms of quality (e.g. better service, output)
and quantity (e.g. more revenue, contracts negotiated) by using less input of resources and by applying time saved towards producing more
and better outputs.

Complementing the notion of efficiency and effectiveness are the concepts of cost displacement and value added. Improvements in efficiency
result in the displacement of costs in a given organization. Improvements
in effectiveness result in adding value. This model of office benefits,
first presented in *Office Automation: A User Driven-Method*, is shown
in Figure 5.3.

Strategy Formulation: Setting Objectives

Once the assessment of global opportunities for improvement has been
completed — essentially by taking stock of the current situation, with its
inherent problems, inefficiencies, limitations, strategies and technological base — the planning group is ready for strategy formulation. This
involves developing a set of objectives for the planning horizon, say, of
three to five years.

The following set of questions, if raised during the planning session,
help to structure and guide the interpretation of, and place the focus on
developing strategy. In some organizations the answers to these questions
and the setting of strategy will be intuitively obvious; in others a great
deal of discussion, and soul-searching may be necessary to arrive at a
coherent strategy and set of objectives.

The case study of the standards organization is used to provide a concrete example of the form these answers might take at the conclusion of
the session.

If we stay the way we are (status quo), where are we going?
For the standards organization, this question was answered by the fact

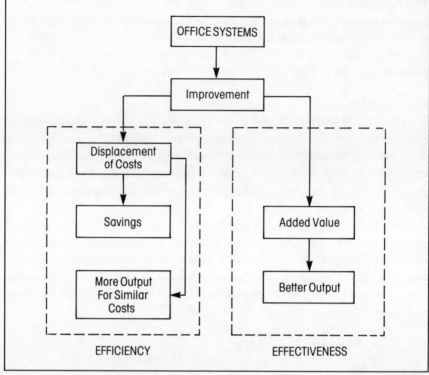

Figure 5.3 Model of Office Benefits

that the organization was finding it increasingly difficult to respond to consumers' needs in a timely, accurate manner. Mounting problems with paper-based systems and the management of information resources had bogged them down in a paper quagmire that was absorbing the energies and destroying the creativity and innovative capabilities of their people. It was no longer a question of continuing with the status quo, but rather a question of how much longer they could survive. The organization was becoming much less of a threat to new and existing competition.

If we change, where are we going?
Again, this question was answered on the basis of having determined a new, emerging mission which could be implemented through the provision of online information products and services which more closely met the needs of their customers. Further, those products and services could be integrated, for the first time, in order to link the standard to the certified product.

Why are we going there?

The answer in this case was ultimately a matter of *survival*, and, it was hoped, furthering the prospects of prosperity.

How will we get there?

In this example, getting there was a matter of continuing the planning process, and implementing a series of "basic building blocks". These included the introduction of technology, changes in job design, organizational structure modification, and changing the process by which the end-products were developed. In effect, rethinking the way they conducted their business, and transforming the business itself.

What is the cost of getting there?

A global view of the relative costs of getting there in this example included the cost of replacing obsolete minicomputers; terminals to support the anticipated user population; office space modifications; furniture; consulting for systems specification, design and implementation; new software to meet functional requirements; and ongoing systems support and maintenance.

What is the benefit of getting there?

In addition to all the long-range strategic benefits, the standards organization identified a number of global cost-displacement and avoidance opportunities. Benefits included the lower cost of a distributed, micro-based system versus a centralized minicomputer system, and the replacement of costly stand-alone word-processing equipment with software included in the overall micro-based system.

There were other savings which could be anticipated, such as a reduction in temporary help, overtime salary costs, consolidation of photocopying with laser printing for an overall lower cost due to bringing those activities in-house. Other examples included the freeing up of physical space through reduction and consolidation of paper-based records. The latter did not amount to a great deal of hard dollars in the bank because square foot space costs were low. However, it meant that they could avoid acquiring additional space to accommodate their current employee population in a reasonable manner.

Other benefits could be categorized as "soft" because they represent savings in time spent on various activities and processes. These could be approximated and integrated into a plan for reinvestment.

Which parts of the organization need to get there first?

Answering this question may be a very difficult process since it involves the choice for initial pilot systems implementations. Often there is competition among the various organizational groups to be first. It is for this reason, that the Strategic Framework has so much importance. The organization's mission, goals and critical success factors should be re-evaluated before attempting to conclude where the pilot systems will be located. Then, the alternatives may be narrowed down to only those groups which are strategic to achievement of these goals. (Other considerations discussed in Chapter Six can also be brought to bear on the selection process.)

Such was the case in the standards organization example. The group responsible for the actual coordination, development and production of the standards was chosen as the prime location for a pilot system. The rationale was that it was the group that could most clearly be impacted by the opportunities while perhaps having the most impact on the new strategic mission.

The relationship of anticipated costs to potential benefits in a one-year scenario and a five-year forecast was formulated. In this example, the costs of the pilot were almost recovered in the initial implementation, with soft benefits growing over time as the user population increased and the system matured. This type of comparison is useful in developing a clear view of the potential impact.

The strategy was then devised and resulted in the following objectives for this organization:

- Enable the Standards Division to better respond to public information demands
- Increase productivity
- Enable professional staff to handle more projects
- Hold constant the physical facilities requirements
- Hold constant the staff complement
- Improve quality of working life and morale
- Project an improved public image
- Continue to provide high quality output
- Enable the organization to compete more effectively
- Afford improvements in existing services
- Facilitate new and expanded products and services.

Strategic Assumptions

A set of operating assumptions should be surfaced as a result of the setting of strategic objectives. These are things which will require senior management sponsorship, commitment and stewardship if the objectives are to be met. Some examples would include assumptions regarding:

- The staffing level, skills, and resources required to implement the plan.
- The feasibility of adopting and implementing policies, standards and procedures for the effective use of technology throughout the organization.
- The ability of the enterprise to implement an effective division of labor and responsibilities regarding systems, including management of the tricky organizational issues.
- The technical feasibility of achieving various levels of systems capability required.
- Commitments to initiate additional studies and programs such as a records management program, which will develop an overall classification scheme, retention and archive schedules, procedures and policies for ongoing maintenance and support.
- The willingness of line management to investigate detailed opportunities within their departments and lead the implementation of strategic pilots.

These are a few examples of the type of assumptions which may need to be stated. The stewarding of these objectives and assumptions is central to successful strategy implementation. The Action Plan discussed in Chapter Thirteen outlines how a project plan for strategic planning and implementation activities over the next year will assist greatly in quantifying and managing these changes.

Reinvestment Model: Repealing Parkinson's Law

As discussed earlier, the main benefits of these new systems lie in time savings — often stemming from streamlining processes, eliminating redundant activities, using the new tools for more efficient information processing and communications, and from redistributing and delegating management and professional activities to administrative personnel.

Saved time does not necessarily translate into improved effectiveness and productivity. Just saving someone an hour a day does not mean that hour will be put to good use — at the individual level. There is little point in saving massive amounts of time across the organization, if it simply dissipates or is lost.

It is through the management of these time savings opportunities that organizations can become better run, more productive, high performers. This is not as difficult as one might imagine. It starts with a simple strategy for the reinvestment of time opportunities at a global level.

The ultimate goal may be to apply more time to the development of *new products* if those that currently exist are nearing the end of their life cycle. It may be to direct more time to *marketing efforts* in order to provide broader coverage of the marketplace, or to expand into new market segments. Time savings for those people who possess important talents, skills and expertise may be a critical success factor in achieving the strategic mission and goals of the enterprise. Regardless, the strategy for initially freeing up time, and channeling that time towards the new direction in a purposeful, constructive manner needs to be developed at this time. An evolutionary approach is required, since there is a certain learning curve in acquiring new ways of working and the skills necessary to effectively use the new tools of knowledge work. This has a natural impact on job content and design, as well as on the procedures and processes that are inherent in our old ways.

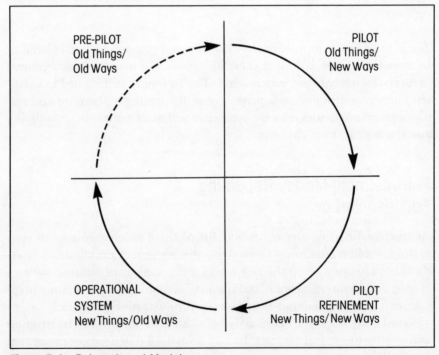

Figure 5.4 Reinvestment Model

The reinvestment model illustrated in Figure 5.4 is useful in describing how time savings can be realized, managed and applied in the directions management feels are most productive. The model shows how time savings can be managed as the enterprise achieves greater maturity vis-a-vis integrated office systems.

Before new pilot systems are introduced, we do *old things* in *old ways*, such as processing memorandums, handwriting and typewriting reports, or manually producing a budget. There is little room for saving time, unless we change things.

After the pilot system is implemented, the focus shifts to doing *old things* in *new ways* with the help of individual tools such as electronic messaging for faster communications, text editors for creative thinking and document production, and electronic spreadsheets to massage, revise and develop budgets. These tools when applied to the old things we do, save us time as we develop experience and skill, and allow us to begin to substitute *new ways* for old.

It is in the third stage, as we reinvest saved time to refine the system and procedures, and develop new applications that combine the previously separate tools and activities, that we can now take on *new things* such as delegated work, projects, reports using new integrated tools or ways. It is the synergy and collective new-found skills applied to existing things that forge the opportunities to do new things, in new ways.

As these systems are extended operationally throughout the organization, we then begin to actually reap the benefits of internally reinvested time savings. The systems and ways are mature, and efficient. They enable us, with our redefined jobs, procedures and processes, to tackle new things at an operational level. The economies of scale are realized, the strategic investment is paying off as we develop new markets, new products, expand our horizons and realize new goals, with the full complement of human resources and operational systems. We then are doing new things in old ways. So we have come full circle.

However, we must not stop here, now that our new ways have become old. We must continually evolve and improve them in order to move forward. The plan, with its existing strategies, goals and assumptions, must be regenerated. New strategies and objectives must be formulated to meet the challenges our reinvestment in expansion and development create. This model depicts a state of creative evolution. It represents a way of looking at the process of managing time savings. Most importantly though, it sets a realistic expectation of what is possible within a given timeframe. Without developing a specific view of how these opportunities will be managed, the global impact of time savings benefits cannot be assessed, the return on strategic investment in systems cannot be determined, and Parkinson's Law will not be repealed.

We'll return to this topic in the last chapter. For now, even as your organization works on the construction of a Strategic Direction, you will need to, simultaneously, begin work on your strategy for *technology* itself. This is the topic of the next five chapters.

TECHNOLOGY STRATEGY

3

The Functional Description and Tools Diffusion Plan

Many traditional systems plans consisted solely of a technology strategy. As is obvious from this book, integrated office systems plans are much more.

Even in the area of technology, a good office systems strategy is likely to be more comprehensive than traditional MIS approaches. A technology strategy is not simply a plan listing the applications which need to be developed in the foreseeable future. Nor is it simply a plan for equipment acquisition. Rather, it should be a complete strategy to develop a coherent technical infrastructure for the organization — based on the strategic direction which has been formulated and consistent with all other "nontechnical" aspects of the plan.

The technology strategy must be driven by the requirements of the users and organization. The various data collection, analysis and discussion activities outlined in the last two chapters will set the initial direction and tone. Note, however that data will continue to be gathered to enable detailed construction of various components of the study.

There are several aspects to a technology strategy, which will be the topics for discussion in these five chapters. They are:

- Functional Description and Tools Diffusion Plan,
- Global Technology Architecture,
- Information Architecture,
- Communications Architecture, and
- Technology Policy.

It should be noted here that these pieces of a technology strategy are not necessarily developed in this order. Because of their interdependency, they will have to be developed more or less simultaneously.

The main tools of integrated office systems have been described in Chapter Two. But how can you get a picture of *which* of these is appropriate, with *what* degree of integration between them, *how* the various pieces can come together, and *when* the various tools should be introduced? The five chapters in this part of the book will help you answer these, and other, vital questions.

Functional Description

At this point, the search for a "Strategic Direction" for integrated systems is well underway. Beyond that, it is necessary to have a more detailed picture of just what the system will actually provide.

A central aspect of this challenge is to identify those tools which have corporate-wide implications. Unless the organization is small it would be a mistake to attempt to develop a detailed design of all aspects of office systems for the enterprise as a whole. The unique requirements of individual departments are best left to the departments to assess and act upon.

One of the important propelling forces behind office systems, especially micro-based systems, is that they can free end-user departments from unnecessary and undesirable centralized control and delay. This is not to say that centralized planning and control is obviated. Indeed the challenge facing senior management is to determine which aspects of a system are best planned centrally and which are best left to end-user departments.

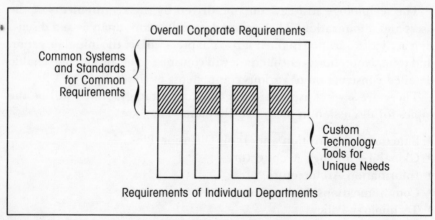

Figure 6.1 Department and Enterprise-Wide Requirements

The relationship between end-user department requirements and enterprise-wide requirements is shown in Figure 6.1. To illustrate a typical enterprise-wide requirement, let's consider *electronic messaging* (both voice and text).

It would be as senseless to have different departments using incompatible messaging systems as it would be to have incompatible telephone systems. Access to the world outside the organization also requires compatability. Until there are widely adopted standards for text and voice messaging, corporate-wide planning is necessary to position the organization to gain access to key persons and organizations outside its walls.

Even when such universal standards are in place planning will still be required to manage the corporate directory, organize corporate filing and archiving of important messages, ensure that there are enough people on the system who have a genuine need to communicate with each other; determine when messaging should be substituted for memos and paper-based communications; develop corporate strategies for reinvestment of the time saved through use of a messaging system and similar concerns. Other corporate-wide requirements include:

- **Access to corporate databases.** This is best planned across the organization, as centralized facilities, communications, access procedures, security, database integrity, and corporate-wide confidentiality of information are involved.
- **Decision support tools.** There is often a requirement to "roll up" financial plans or budgets across the enterprise. Where such requirements don't exist and are unlikely to develop, it may make sense to leave such applications to individual departments.
- **Meeting scheduling.** A corporate-wide scheduling system can be beneficial, but must be planned accordingly. For similar reasons, it may make sense to apply a common project-management method across the enterprise and plan a corporate-wide system tool to facilitate project management.

On the other hand, there are a number of tools which are usually best left to the individual department to plan. Typically, these are tools which do not require corporate-wide facilities or communications. For example:

- **Text processing.** This can often be left to the end-user group, in particular where document distribution requirements do not extend beyond the given department. In some cases, it may however, be desirable to implement corporate plans and standards for document distribution.
- **Specialized applications.** Typical examples are scientific applications, unique data processing applications or management graphics required by a given department.
- **Isolated communications tools.** For example a mail-log tool might help a given department track and manage paper-based mail even when there are not corporate-wide requirements for channeling or tracking

mail. An example of this would be the case of a large government department which had a need to manage correspondence sent to the elected official and channeled throughout the department.

In the long run we anticipate a trend towards the use of tools which enable corporate-wide compatibility and standardization. One part of the art of planning is to balance the long-term utility of such corporate-wide standardization with the genuine and legitimate short-term needs of end-user groups for tools which are useful within the framework of their own group.

Functional Description for a Large Retail Company

The following Functional Description was taken from the executive summary of an office systems strategic plan of a large retail company. (The complete description was more detailed, and outlined the features required of each tool to enable full utility and usability as well as the functional integration required between tools.)

The company had already formulated a Strategic Framework and Strategic Direction which focused on the need to be a high performance organization which could quickly identify and respond to changes in the marketplace. Implementation of multifunction workstations for office personnel, linked to other technologies, such as point of sale and warehouse systems, was judged to be critical to success.

Based on the company-wide examination of our office system requirements for the next five to ten years, it is both feasible and prudent to implement workstations for most groups of our office personnel ... At the end of the first strategic planning horizon, workstations should be delivering the following functionality:

1. **Communications:** A corporate-wide text and voice messaging system will give all office personnel, including management in the plants and warehouses, asynchronous access to each other and, through an interface to a public messaging network, to the branch offices in all countries where we are located. Internal paper-based memos will be eliminated over this time-frame through messaging and a corporate-wide document distribution system. We will provide all head office personnel with access to the new telephone features of a third generation PBX. Audio teleconferencing will be implemented for all second level managers and above, and each regional office will have a special teleconferencing room with slow-scan facilities.

2. **Information Resource Functions:** All executive management will have on-line access to a variety of important corporate databases. Such access will

be "read only" in the form of videotex graphic output. All employees will have access to public databases to enable capabilities such as airline reservation scheduling, review of stock markets, access to public affairs data; electronic filing and group databases are left to the discretion of individual divisions and departments.

3. Financial Planning Tools: All managers will be given access to standardized spreadsheet tools for budgeting. These tools will enable the aggregation of budget information both across the company (internationally) and historically (over time). More sophisticated statistical analysis tools, currently running in batch mode on the head office mainframes will be made available in interactive mode to those who require them.

4. Time and Resource Management: The (company) project management system will be moved online and project planning, tracking and control tools will be made availabe to all project managers and all other second level managers and above. Video projectors will be available in one boardroom in each location where there are monthly project reviews. These will eliminate all paper in the project management process and also eliminate the construction of summary presentation material for these meetings.

The board memo process (for construction of memos for capital expenditures to be considered by the monthly meetings of the Board of Directors) will be streamlined and based on a electronic memo linked to the project management system. Additionally, meetings of all senior personnel, above third level, will be scheduled using an online scheduling system and require the use of electronic calendars.

5. System Accounting and Monitoring: A full range of system accounting and administration tools will be implemented for system billing, diagnosis, evaluation, password maintenance, system support, etc.

6. User Training Facilities: A "tutorial" package will be available to all new users. It will enable proficiency in all company-wide applications as well as other basic system skills such as using a printer, generating graphics from various databases and archiving files.

Tools Diffusion Plan

Once a detailed Functional Description that outlines what the system will deliver to the end-user has been constructed, it is necessary to develop a plan regarding how these tools will be diffused across the organization. Such a plan indicates the most desirable scenario, based on (a) the *need* for the enterprise to have access to such tools and (b) on a first cut at the *feasibility* of proceeding with various scenarios. However, it should be noted that a complete plan for how these tools will be sequenced across the enterprise is not possible until an overall systems architecture has been formulated. This is the topic of the next two chapters.

Tools Diffusion Plan for a Large Manufacturing Company

What would a Tools Diffusion Plan look like for the large retail company discussed previously? The most appropriate way to phase-in the tools chosen in the company's Functional Description appeared to be an implementation strategy of several phases. The following outline of the plan was contained in the executive summary to the office systems strategic plan

Phase I: During Phase I we undertake the simultaneous implementation of:

- text messaging across the existing terminal base;
- a standardized spreadsheet tool for designated managers.

Phase II:
- A company-wide common user interface, portable to all designated personal computers, minicomputers and central mainframes; to include standardized help facilities and training programs;
- system accounting tools to measure use of various tools from this common interface shell;
- a corporate-wide document distribution system, utilizing the teletex standard;
- a third generation PBX in the head office building, providing audio conferencing, enhanced telephone and access to voice messaging;
- corporate use by managers of electronic calendars and a meeting scheduling system;
- statistical packages (SPSS and SAS) in an interactive mode.

Phase III:
- Construction of interfaces to selected corporate financial databases for senior management, including videotex graphic display and interaction;
- implementation of the company project management system online, including installation of video projectors;
- links between the project management system and the memo process, coupled with a redesign of the board memo process to enable online processing and tracking of board memos;
- the online "tutorial" package to enable user competence with company-wide tools and familiarity with the user interface.

Sequencing Entry Pilots

The world of office automation has come full circle on the debate over strategy *within a given department* (as opposed to the organization as a whole). A few years ago the generally accepted strategy in advanced organizations was the "pilot approach". User requirements within a given department were assessed in some form of feasibility study and requirements analysis and a pilot group selected. A system was specified, a vendor was selected, a system was implemented and evaluated, and the pilot, if successful, was extended to a full operational system. There were several rationales for this approach:

- It is not wise, appropriate or possible to implement full operational systems. Rather, it makes sense to start with a pilot where the department can get its feet wet; make some mistakes and learn from them; evaluate and refine the system and then, based on experience, extend the pilot to an operational system.
- It is important to have a user-driven approach to office systems, where the needs of the department and its people, not technology, drive the design process.
- Information to perform a cost-benefit analysis must be collected, given that a complete pilot "system" — usually minicomputer-based — is a substantial investment.

For a brief time in the early 1980s the pilot was forgotten. The recession forced many organizations to focus on cost-avoidance applications of computer technology, resulting in slow growth of office mini- and mainframe-based office automation pilots which tended to have "soft" or value-added benefits. Simultaneously, the introduction of the micro into business — especially second generation 16-bit micros and more especially the IBM PC — created what appeared to be a low risk, low profile, low cost, low disruption entry point for office automation. For a few thousand dollars, well within the discretionary budgets of hundreds of thousands of managers, a department could go beyond word processing and get a multifunctional tool on the desks of professionals and managers and other departmental personnel.

However, the massive problems with this approach have begun to surface in organizations across North America. Many, if not most, of micros in the office were simply not used, or used only for brief, infrequent periods. Without some kind of departmental plan, the functionality provided by micros was limited primarily to spreadsheet applications. Key tools such as electronic messaging or user-friendly access to other computer resources — for example, corporate databases — was not possible. The thrust of the micro was to support only the *individual* rather than the *work group*. As such, the micro couldn't support the individual in critical work activities which involve communication.

Because there had been no attention paid to the social issues (procedures, job design, responsibilities, etc.) or to the changes required in the work environment, many problems arose which hurt user-acceptance of micros. On top of this, each user often used different software packages, having different interfaces and requiring specialized and non-standardized training. Add to this the fact that most micro software had quite inadequate user documentation and training packages and you'll understand why the under-utilized or dormant micro often became the norm rather than the exception.

At the same time, many senior managers were becoming concerned about their organization groping their way into the information age through the unplanned creation of a corporate technical infrastructure based on micros. As a result, overall strategic planning for integrated systems moved to center stage.

So today, in advanced organizations, there is a clear shift back towards more departmental pilots. These pilots, however, are now *designed* within the framework of an overall corporate strategic plan for integrated office systems. Today's pilots differ from those of the 1970s in that they take advantage of the personal computer, but, unlike the previous wave of groping with micros, are more conscious *projects*, *with objectives*, *a clear project plan*, milestones, assigned resources and an evaluation.

A Tools Diffusion Plan should contain strategy regarding the initiation and extension of such pilots.

Criteria for Selecting a Pilot

The success or failure of your first entry pilot will establish or destroy the credibility of those involved, determine the atmosphere for implementations, set the stage for the extension of the pilot to operational systems, and of course have a crucial impact on the performance of the department in question. For these reasons, it makes sense to take some time to ensure that the right pilot group is selected — one that will provide a fair test of the probability of success.

In addition to identifying global opportunities for corporate-wide technologies, information from the corporate-wide Opportunity Analysis can be used to help select the first (or next) entry pilot. Typically, a pilot is located within one department of the organization. It usually begins with a group of ten to forty people, who each receive an electronic workstation.

Most pilots require four to ten months from the time of implementation. At the end of that period a decision is usually made on whether or not the pilot should be expanded.

Sometimes the introduction of several stand-alone personal computers is considered to be a "pilot". We have found, however that such initial experiments are limited in their impact and in the lessons they can provide. Rather, high leverage pilots usually involve communication among people and devices in the pilot group and to people and devices outside the pilot group, such as to the mainframe or to a public messaging system.

A structured discussion among participants in the planning process can be used to establish certain *criteria* for selecting a pilot. This can help ensure that the pilot selected meets the organization's clearly defined needs. It may also be desirable to involve representatives from various candidate departments in such a discussion. Selection of a pilot can be a tricky business, involving the personal and political interests of various managers. Establishing clear criteria can make the actual selection of a pilot less subjective and arbitrary.

One of our clients, a large insurance company, had several hundred microcomputers throughout the organization. It decided to select one department, assess requirements, perform a feasibility analysis, select a vendor, implement and evaluate the pilot. If successful, the pilot would be extended to an operational integrated office system. The criteria were hammered out in a couple of workshops, and each weighted as to its importance. After the Opportunity Analysis had been completed, a short list of pilots was drafted and each pilot was scored on each of the criteria. The criteria "weights" were used to adjust each pilot's scores accordingly.

It was interesting that the company did not choose the pilot which scored the highest, but one which was a close second. After seeing the scores those involved they went back and re-evaluated the criteria and decided that a refinement was in order. This may appear as evidence for the First Law of Pilot Selection: "The probability of you selecting a certain pilot group is directly proportional to the degree to which you thought it was a good idea anyway." A less cynical commentator might conclude that the process simply provided a structure and procedure for discussing and resolving the matter.

Here is a summary of the criteria from the company's draft Strategic Plan for Integrated Office Systems.

1. **User Need**: The first criterion for selecting a pilot is that the group must have substantial requirements to use office systems. The real opportunity must be substantial.

2. **Support of the Pilot Group Management for the Project**: It is essential that the unit management are fully supportive of the pilot, and committed to freeing adequate personnel, time and resources to enable a successful implementation.

3. **Attitude of the Pilot Group Itself**: Our first pilot, to be low risk, must consist of people who are supportive of the project; willing to make it work; open to using a networked personal computer as part of their job; and who have a *felt* need to see their unit improved, in addition to a real need.

4. **Visibility**: We don't want our first pilot to necessarily be highly visible, yet is should not be a marginal group. It is important that a successful pilot not be discounted as marginal or outside the mainstream of the business.

5. **Cost**: While cost is not our highest consideration, it is desirable that the pilot system be low cost. This will benefit those units which already have a number of 16 and 32 bit micros which can be networked into a pilot configuration.

6. **Minimal Development Requirements**: It is important that the pilot selected can be ``off-the-shelf'' technology, rather than one which requires considerable application development by the Electronic Data Processing Division. Delays in implementation increase the risk of the loss of support by the target user group.

7. **Minimal Disruption**: It is important that the detailed feasibility study and pretest we will conduct in the pilot group, along with the implementation itself, not create undue disruption to the work of the unit. We have a business to run here and the transition to the pilot system must be smooth.

8. **Measureability**: We would prefer to have a pilot group which is involved in activities and which produces products which are reasonably easy to measure. This will help us understand what impacts on productivity were achieved and also provide the evidence for the business case to extend the pilot to a production system for the unit as a whole.

9. **Size**: Seeing as we want to include text messaging in any pilot we conduct, it is essential that the pilot group is large enough to generate a reasonable level of messaging activity.

Corporate-Wide Technologies:
Where To Start

As noted earlier in this chapter, we can't really deal with the issue of how to sequence corporate-wide technologies, such as electronic messaging and access to corporate databases, until we have an overall system architecture. To develop this part of a plan we first have to have some other pieces of the puzzle in place. This is the topic of the next two chapters.

Global Technology Architecture

In our experience, many non-technical managers have some difficulty with the notion of a technology "architecture". Much of the confusion originates from the fact that the term has been used in many different ways. For example, one vendor alone — IBM — has used many different denotations of the term in its literature and marketing materials. The company has developed the notions of an "Information Architecture", "Systems Network Architecture", "Document Content Architecture", and "Document Interchange Architecture".

The concept of an architecture, or various types of architectures, however, is a good one, although it could benefit from clarification and standardization.

An architecture is best viewed as a high-level specification of the structure of a system. From the perspective of developing an overall technology strategy, three related architectures must be developed. A *Global Technology Architecture* is an overall description of the structure of technology within the organization. It outlines how computer intelligence is to be distributed throughout the enterprise. An *Information Architecture* maps out how information will be organized, processed and distributed. A *Communications Architecture* is a specification of network structures that will enable appropriate levels of communications within the enterprise and without. This last architecture includes the high-level rules, or protocols, to be followed by devices on the network.

Drafting a Global Technology Architecture

A plan is required outlining how the technology will be structured throughout the organization. This requires both a basic configuration and a plan for how that arrangement will, or may, evolve with time, given certain foreseeable scenarios for the organization as a whole. A good architecture will, among other things, correspond to the nature and requirements of the organization even as the organization changes and grows.

For the ancient Greeks, an architecture was fundamentally an expression of a set of values. So it is with an overall technology architecture. The distribution of computer intelligence, or processing power, as well as the corresponding software, reflect the nature of that enterprise and its management.

Consider how, in the archetypal "highly centralized" organization, most decisionmaking of any significance is done at the top. Most requirements for information are by senior management at head office. There is little delegation of authority. Communications channels tend to be vertical. In such an organization (all other things being equal), one could argue for a highly central architecture in which most of the system intelligence is in a centralized computer facility. In the case of a company headquartered in New York and having branch offices in Chicago, Toronto and Los Angeles, a large mainframe computing facility could be located in the head office building with access through "dumb" terminals in that building and remote locations.

At the other extreme, a federation of small businesses may have highly distributed authority, decisionmaking and control. Information requirements are somewhat unique to each, with some requirements for passing information between member businesses. A technology architecture for such an organization would likely be highly decentralized with computer processing primarily resident in each of the end-user companies.

In both cases, the architecture would suit the values, decisionmaking process, authority, information-handling and organizational communications relationships of the enterprise.

In the early days of computer systems all architectures were centralized due to the cost of the technology, the batch-oriented applications for which computers were used and the immaturity of computer networking. Large organizations, who were the only ones who could afford in-house computer facilities typically had one or more large "mainframe" computers locked up in a "data center". To use computing facilities, "jobs" were submitted, first on punch cards and later on magnetic tapes, by technically-skilled operators, programmers and other data processing personnel. Typical output was the company payroll, a listing of accounts receivable or the general ledger.

In the 1970s we saw the advent of the mini-computer and with it the growth of distributed data processing (DDP). Computers were becoming less expensive, smaller and could be hooked together using various kinds of communications networks. While there was still a major role for the large mainframe (which continued to grow in capacity and speed in the context of a rapidly expanding market for computer technology in general), the power of the corporate computer system began to move closer to the end-user. For example, data-processing applications required in the regional office could be done by a mini-computer located there. Information required for corporate processing and decisionmaking could be aggregated and passed on through the network to the central mainframe computing facility.

If the 1970s was the decade of the mini, the 1980s will most likely be known as the decade of the micro. First introduced in the latter half of the 1970s, the personal computer, was originally targeted at the hobbyist market. Scorned by many data-processing managers as toys, the first generation of micros (with an internal address size of 8 bits) such as the Apple II and TRS-80 soon began to find its way into business. Software packages such as the Visicalc electronic spreadsheet provided useful functionality to end-users who were often fed up with waiting a year or two (or sometimes more) for the data-processing department to develop an application program for their needs. With the introduction of the second generation of micros (having an internal address size of 16 bits), in particular the first IBM Personal Computer, the micro explosion was detonated.

During the late 1970s there was also widespread growth of word processing. Originally conceived, marketed and implemented as a stand-alone device for reducing clerical costs through improved typing efficiency, word processing has begun to disappear as a separate technology. Text-editing capabilities have been integrated into minicomputer-based integrated office systems at the high end. At the low end, micros acquired word-processing capabilities. In general, however, computing capacity was moving even closer to the end-user.

Ever since the first days of distributed data processing there has been an ongoing debate over centralization versus decentralization of computing resources. Clearly the decision on which way to go has been an important one for many organizations, even before the rise of integrated office systems. Typical considerations include:

1. Geographical Dispersion
Decentralized systems are often more appropriate for organizations which are widely distributed, lowering communications costs and possibly enabling a faster response time for end-users.

2. Nature of the Application(s)
Distributed systems often lend themselves better to interactive processing, rather than batch applications. They can also be more appropriate when

there are particular end-user requirements. Rather than adjusting the special needs of various branches or departments of an organization to the centralized system, it may make sense to have distributed, local processing. Field information required by head office can then be extracted and aggregated centrally.

3. Capacity Requirements
Sometimes the processing requirements are simply too large to be effectively handled by one central computer alone. This may be true when there is a particularly complex database, an inordinately large volume of transactions to be processed, or a very large user population who need online access to computing facilities.

4. Requirements for Expandability
In making the case for a distributed approach to systems, Xerox Corporation developed the notion of the "agony and ecstasy" of computer expansion. As the tale goes, when the VP of Systems is in agony, the VP of Finance is in ecstasy — and vice versa. That is, when the system is badly overloaded and the Systems VP is suffering the Finance VP is pleased to see there haven't been any major computer expenditures of late. However, when the situation is resolved by purchasing another large, centralized and under utilized computer, the Systems VP is delighted with the extra capability and the Finance VP stings from the cost. The moral of the story is that if expansion is seen as likely, distributed processing may enable a more incremental growth of systems.

5. Requirements for Flexibility
Centralized databases can be very complex and difficult to change. If requirements for changes to the system are anticipated, distribution may be more appropriate.

6. Development Risk
While centralized systems can be a major development challenge, they tend to be better known quantities than highly distributed systems. The inertia of traditional data-processing education and experience, coupled with the newness of distributed systems has resulted in centralized systems generally being lower-risk — at least when it comes to traditional DP applications.

7. Requirements for Reliability and Availability
Centralized systems are more vulnerable to catastrophic failure, although there ways to ensure system availability. The most common safeguard is

to use redundant hardware, either providing the failsafe type or simply duplicating hardware resources. In decentralized systems, the requirements for up-time can be customized to the appropriate user groups, including those in different time zones.

8. Security Requirements
In addition to reliability, protection of a system from unauthorized use is usually an important requirement. It is easier to secure centralized systems by restricting physical access to the computing facilities. Distributed systems may be partitioned to ensure that data or sites which have high security requirements can be protected.

9. Cost
Whether a distributed or centralized route is more cost effective will be a function of the preceding issues as well as others. These include the costs of maintenance, systems support, distributing programming expertise, training costs, facilities costs for computer rooms, wiring, building services and costs of supplies.

The advent of microcomputers and integrated office systems has altered this picture somewhat, although many of the basic considerations stay the same. Today, generic tools which require no formal application development and which lend themselves well to desktop processing can address many requirements. Good examples are decision support, text processing, computer graphics and database management tools. The dramatic growth of micro capacity that is projected to continue also indicates that end-users will be supported by much more direct computing capacity. Statements such as "within a few short years the largest mainframes of today will be on the desktop" began in the late seventies. Not only have such statements proven true, but it is anyone's guess as to when or if they will cease to be valid.

Case Study

In 1981 the Exxon Research and Engineering Company drafted a "Corporate Services' Plan for Automated Information, Office and Computing Systems". The plan grappled with the problem of overall technology architecture, discussing the merits of a mainframe, mini- and microcomputer approaches to providing personal computing cabilities to end-users. The following excerpts provide a helpful guide to the strengths and weaknesses of various approaches to technology architecture. The excerpts also describe well the dilemma faced by the company at the same time. While highly distributed micro-based solutions have many advantages, the technology for networking such systems was then in its early stages.

Corporate Services Plan

Mainframe Computer Approach

Mainframes fall short of office systems and end-user service. Office system packages on mainframes have not provided commercial-grade, easy-to-use text editing. The text editing they do provide requires patience on the part of a user and a great deal of start-up time to learn. These learning curves are tolerated by professional programmers but not by non-programmers.

There are three other drawbacks to a mainframe system. As one loads more applications on a mainframe, response time can become erratic and extremely slow. Also, if the main processor has a problem, all users of the system are unable to use it until it is fixed. Finally, mainframes are inherently difficult to augment in a graceful manner. They tend to be over-configured when first installed then underconfigured as use increases. Capacity must be increased in large blocks rather than in gradual, smooth increases.

In ER&E (Exxon Research and Engineering) where the user environment is continually changing, this is a serious drawback. The system cannot be re-configured until there are sufficient numbers to warrant it. This means it can never grow at incremental rates without trading off service. Ultimately, system growth in a large, centralized mainframe environment must come in large chunks.

Minicomputer Approach

Minicomputers, on the other hand, provide a more flexible growth environment. System resources can be more smoothly and cost-effectively added when demand changes. Because a minicomputer is generally dedicated to an individual group, the minicomputer can be highly responsive to that group's needs.

Minicomputers, however seem to have most of the bad points of the mainframe with few of the good points. Minicomputers are scaled down versions of mainframes; in particular minis use the same relatively slow communications mechanisms. As a result, minis can rarely achieve the file and peripheral sharing, communications and connectivity that are required of a truly integrated environment.

No vendor offers all the functions that ER&E needs, and it is unrealistic to expect, based on what is available today (1981), that total (mini-based) software packages, marketed through third party vendors, will supply all of ER&E's integrated-office needs.

Microcomputer (Personal Computer) Approach

Personal Computers . . . take distribution one step further. They provide a dedicated processor to every user. This means that it is literally available at all times and that the user is virtually independent of all others. With the addition of a fast, local network to interconnect personal computers, the communications and file-and-device-sharing problems of minicomputers are solved.

The potential this offers is great. First, as each new system user is identified, a computer can be incrementally supplied at incremental cost. Thus, a system can grow and continually be reconfigured as demand warrants.

The more diverse the applications mix, the more practical a personal computer. Any new application does not present a drain on shared resources because all users have their own processors. In ER&E, this is an extremely important consideration because our user environment is so diverse.

To date (1981), microprocessor-based systems have not been an overall solution to integrated office, computing and information needs. They have failed in precisely the areas where mainframes succeeded, namely massive file storage, file sharing, connectivity, software, number crunching and economies of scale for expensive peripherals. This, however, will change as local networks become available. . . .

Couple local networks with a microprocessor-based system, and one can provide local computing power to the end-user. This capability can expand and contract with users' needs. Each processor can be tailored to the users' needs, and users can enjoy response times corresponding to the complexity of their applications.[1]

Planning for Hybrid, Multi-level Architectures

Some clear trends are emerging which help provide a direction for long-range strategy for global technology architecture.

1. TREND: the overall intelligence of systems is moving closer to the desktop

Continuing advances in microprocessor technology and the plummeting costs of micros greatly enhance the ability to deliver the computing capacity required for integrated office systems cost-effectively to the desktop.

Integrated office systems require this kind of capacity for three reasons. First, the functionality of office systems needs considerable computing power. Tools like spreadsheets, text processing and computer graphics tend to work best when each user has a dedicated machine. With traditional centralized architectures, the screen can be updated only as fast as the communications line permits. Often this is simply too slow for a personal workstation, where the user may want to refresh a spreadsheet, insert a word into some text or change a bar graph to a pie chart on the screen. Add to this the problems of degradation in response time if many people are using the system as well as large communications costs for remote use of a centralized facility and the case is clear.

Second, to make a system easy-to-use for the non-technical user, considerable computing power is required. Office personnel require a responsive, flexible, natural language interface. Graphic displays using pictorial images on the screen, such as icons or multiple windowing that allow the user to do more than one thing on the screen (just as he or she would do more than one thing on a desktop) are basic requirements for a good interface.

Third, normal use of an office system soon generates massive requirements for local storage. A typical user may generate several dozen text messages, thousands of numbers, a variety of graphics, and many pages of textual information in one week. Add to this the requirements for storing digitized voice, and it is clear that local storage requirements are considerable.

2. TREND: Requirements for centralized or shared computing facilities will not disappear in the future

Rather, personal microcomputers are increasingly being *networked* into complex communications networks which enable people to communicate with other resources and with other people. The trend to desktop intelligence does not obviate the need for central resources as some have argued.[2] Advances in microchip technology which have propelled the personal computer also apply to larger computers. While some uses of mainframe computers, such as bureaus who rent computing power to end-users, are quickly disappearing, there are others that are more enduring. A good example is the finance industry, whose growing requirements for huge, complex and highly secure databases do not lend themselves well to current distributed database technology. As costs drop for large computers and their capacity grows, they should play an increased role in manufacturing, retail and wholesale sectors.

Consequently networks are becoming a critical and central part of the picture. Complex multi-level networks enable communications between computers of varying sizes, types and locations. Added to this is a clear trend to the interconnection of devices from more than one vendor by building "open networks" which have network protocols, or rules, regarding use of the network and access of other facilities.

Networks are also becoming *hybrid*, involving many different media (data, text, voice and image), topologies (star, ring, bus, tree, etc.), transmission media (coaxial cable, twisted pair telephone wires, fiber optics, infra-red light, radio, etc.) and protocols (the rules governing access and use of the network by devices on it). One particularly important development is that the corporate telephone switch or PBX (private branch exchange) is becoming a computer. As such the PBX can act as a key part of the computer network, switching digitized information other than voice.

3. TREND: There is a growing need for corporate database planning

Many have argued the opposite, but circumstances are proving them wrong. It was thought that the growth of micros as well as the rise of office systems in general would provide generic information-handling tools which would bypass traditional management information systems. Structured information, which was the domain of MIS, was said to be less important than the semi-structured and unstructured decisionmaking addressed by the new technology.[3] This view was reinforced by many hardware vendors who encouraged users to purchase and install off-the-shelf technology and worry about how these would fit with the corporate information resource at a later date.

The opposite is the case. Any workstation which addresses generic functions such as text messaging, spreadsheet calculating or word processing, quickly raises broader issues regarding the enterprise's databases. On-line access to structured information in the corporate database seems a natural. What happens when you want to consolidate the results of various departmental budgets in spreadsheet format, and later, track the results against actuals? Moreover, as technology begins to change the work *process*, issues of what data will be used, by whom, at what points, become sharply posed.

Add to this the new database management systems (DBMS), which require considerable thought and preparation to implement, and it is apparent that constructing a coherent "Information Architecture" becomes more important as technology proliferates.

Keeping these trends in mind, the job is to design a Global Technology Architecture based on the nature of the organization, the Strategic Framework which has been determined, the Strategic Direction which has been adopted, and the other components of the technology strategy.

Figure 7.1 illustrates how a Global Technology Architecture might be pictured.

The organization depicted in Figure 7.1 can be described in terms of four levels: the individual, work group, department and enterprise. A Global Technology Architecture must enable the delivery of corporate-wide functionality to end-users, while providing each user, work group and department with the ability to define unique needs and implement technologies which can meet those needs.

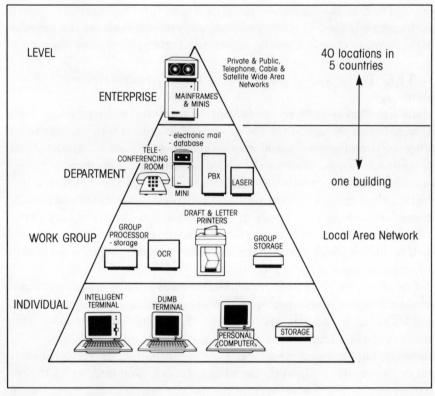

Figure 7.1 A Global Technology Architecture

In the case illustrated , the individual has access to a personal workstation with *hard disk storage*. The work group has certain resources which it members share through a local area network (LAN) and a PBX. Individuals and work groups within each department have access to each other and departmental resources through the PBX located in that building and through a hierarchy of multi-level LANs, depending on the kind and volume of the information (voice, data, text or image) to be communicated. Finally, all have access to other persons and resources in the enterprise through wide area networks.

Here are some examples of how the architecture works:

- A user sends a text message. The message passes up through the work group and department LAN and, not yet finding the recipient, passes on to the corporate network and corporate-wide directory.
- A senior manager asks for a consolidation of current budgets by calling a program at her workstation. This program allows the mainframe

computer in turn to query all departmental systems for the latest budget figures that have been aggregated from work group managers.

- A secretary requests the next available time for meeting of a group of managers. A calendar program searches a hierarchy of calendars, which goes as high as the department level, before all attendees are identified and a time is found.
- Two professionals from different work groups within one department discuss common information on their workstation screens while using the telephone. The PBX switches the voice and data simultaneously.
- A full corporate-wide meeting of all managers is held using the teleconferencing facilities on each floor of each building. A LAN networks these facilities together within the building and provides access to the public telephone and satellite systems.

This example is representative of a medium-to-large organization. However, the same general principles hold true for a smaller enterprise where individuals are grouped in work groups and departments. So the same guidelines would apply to constructing a Global Technology Architecture that can enable the realization of the company's Strategic Direction for integrated systems.

Any organization, regardless of size, can benefit from the general trend of bring technology in tune with the most well-managed, excellent, organizations. From a broader philosophical perspective, it is worthwhile to note that

- In such organizations human intelligence is distributed throughout the organization and human information processing is critical to the organization's success.
- The people in the organization also communicate with each other through complex human communication networks which are hybrid and multi-level.
- As well, information is becoming more important to individuals and collecting, analyzing and sharing that information is critical to individual and organizational performance.

In any event, before a Global Technology Architecture can be formulated, it is necessary to collect some additional information and to conduct some further analytical activities. Which leads us to the next chapter.

Information Architecture

In many ways, a blueprint for the information resource is the foundation of a technology strategy for integrated office systems. This "Information Architecture" refers to a description or structuring of critical, or strategic corporate information. Such a structure must be designed before an overall office systems structure or Global Technology Architecture can be formulated.

The Information Architecture must describe further how information will be distributed throughout the organization. As this picture evolves, indicating what information will be managed at which level (corporate, departmental, workgroup and individual), it in turn establishes the requirements for how processing power must be distributed. It also helps to determine the types of hardware and software that will be required.

Information Resources Management (IRM) is a concept which first became popular in the late 1970s among data processing and MIS managers. IRM holds that as intangible as information may be, and as difficult to measure, it is just as much a corporate resource as are human, material and financial resources, and should be managed as such.

Information can exist in various forms — written, spoken, graphic, pictorial, electronic. It can sometimes be found and evaluated conveniently; at other times, it is not clear what information is required, let alone where it can be located. All the same, this elusive commodity called information allows us to plan our strategies, carry out our operations, monitor our progress against objectives, identify emerging problems and opportunities, formulate appropriate offensive and defensive actions and report on our activities to our various stakeholders.

Contrary to popular belief, information is not a free good. It costs to collect it in the first place, and these costs increase as it is processed, disseminated and ultimately disposed of. There is a cost associated with not having information, at the right time, the right place, or in the right form. Conversely, a value or premium can be assigned to the availability of integrated and compatible processing facilities. As a consequence, policies, standards and guidelines must be in place to ensure the effective management of this resource.

Like IRM, the notion of an Information Architecture has its origins in data processing and management information systems. As computer systems became widespread during the early 1970s the concept of establishing a consistent structure for the corporate information and data resources became popular, and with good reason.

For example, financial systems such as payroll or accounts receivable are usually quite highly defined. Typically a data element — such as employee — has been defined, along with a variety of attributes (such as number, name, rate, hours and deductions). The element and attributes are unlikely to change over time, although the applications for the information might change and vary. Besides payroll (which itself can go through a few generations of software and hardware), the employee record might be used for such applications as personnel planning or stock option plans. The various applications which need the employee information may all refer back to the same database. Or, each application designer may create a unique record structure which is incompatible with the others. The result: redundant file structures with inconsistent information, and in general, an information resource which lacks accuracy, accessibility and usefulness.

During the late 1970s, defining the information architecture became even more important as database systems became popular and were implemented in smaller distributed computers as well as larger machines.

The increasing popularity of the personal computer exacerbated any problems and caused a few new ones. Unplanned databases on microcomputers have led to the duplication of data; the undermining of the integrity of data input to the central database; the problem of "copy management" as information from corporate databases was downloaded to local desktop microcomputers, copied and changed; the problem of determining the existence of databases, and documenting data; problems of confidentiality, security, back-up, recovery, and in general an enhanced need for database planning and data management.

For many organizations, these problems become highly visible during the initiation of integrated office systems planning and implementation of the first entry pilots. Office system pilots are often situated within the context of a traditional Information Architecture. As the local or departmental databases are built up on the office systems pilot, the question quickly arises: "How do these databases fit into the overall Information Architecture?"

It is important to recognize that the use of electronic workstations by growing numbers of office personnel raises information issues which go beyond corporately owned, computerized information. Specifically, executives, managers, professionals and other office employees require access to external private and public databases, as well as internal and external information which is not in computer form. All information sources are critical to decisionmaking in an automated environment and become considerations for information resource planning.

As an overall map of the structure and distribution of information, an architecture is, in effect, an informational mirror of the organization. It reflects planning, development, production, distribution and accounting of goods and services. It includes the range of organizational resources from people to capital goods. It encompasses both computer and non-computer sources. Most important, it is designed to enable the effective management and use of that key resource: information itself.

Design Methodologies

Information Architecture is a relatively young discipline. It has evolved from methods put forward by IBM under the Business Systems Planning framework. New approaches, best typified by the work of computer consultant James Martin, emerged early in the 1980s. Today, the perspective of integrated office systems provides some additional solutions. To understand how these differ, it is important to first review the two previous main approaches.

Business Systems Planning

IBM defines Business Systems Planning (BSP) as a structured approach to helping an organization establish an information systems plan that can satisfy its near- and long-term information needs and is part of the overall business plan.[1]

The basic concepts of Business Systems Planning reflect IBM's view of the long-term objectives for information systems in an organization:

- An information system must support the goals and objectives of the business.
- An information system strategy should address the needs of all levels of management in the business.
- An information system should provide consistency of information throughout the organization.
- An information system should be able to survive through organizational and management change.

- The information system strategy should be implemented by subsystems within a total Information Architecture.[2]

The last point acknowledges the fact that it is not possible for a single information system to support the entire business unit's needs. What IBM advocates is top-down information system planning with bottom-up implementation. Identified systems are implemented in a modular, building-block fashion over time, while remaining consistent with the organization's business priorities, available funds, and other shorter-term considerations.

Business Systems Planning provides a detailed methodology for study, analysis and design. Such a study begins with top management sponsorship and executive involvement. Key steps are then as follows:

- **Defining business processes.** The range of business functions and activities are listed and those which are critical to the success of the business are identified. Processes are defined as groups of logically related decisions and activities required to manage the resources of the business.
- **Defining data classes.** *A data class is a category of logically related data.* The classification is aimed at helping the business develop databases with a minimum of redundancy and in a manner which allows systems to be added without a major revision to the databases.
- **Analyzing current systems support.** Business processes and data classes are mapped against each other and against computer applications and business departments. (The main tool of analysis is a series of matrices which are shown in IBM's BSP manual.) Relationships, redundancies and gaps are identified.
- **Determining the executive perspective.** This is a critical part of the study. IBM provides detailed methods and instruments for executive interviews. The purpose is to validate the work of the team and provide the business understanding necessary for information systems planning.
- **Defining findings and conclusions.** These are summarized and categorized. Non-DP problems are forwarded to management.
- **Defining Information Architecture.** This is the major output of the study, and is explained in more detail below.

To define the Information Architecture, data classes are placed in a matrix opposite the business processes. Processes are listed according to the life-cycle sequence of the company's product (see Figure 8.1). Data classes are listed in sequence by the process creating the data. The letters *C* and *U* are entered in the matrix to indicate which processes create the data

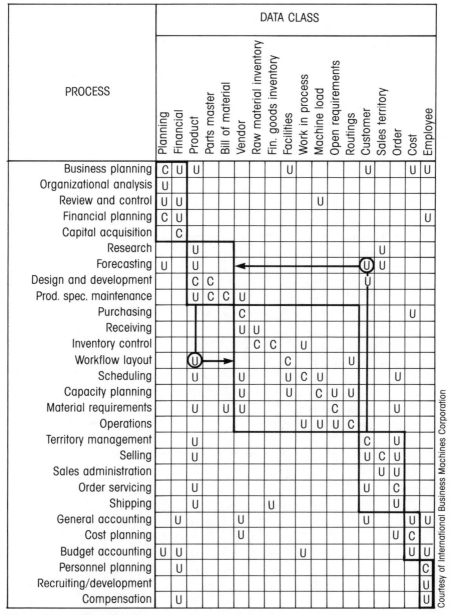

Figure 8.1   IBM BSP Data Classes versus Processes

and which use it. When properly arranged (or rearranged) the Cs will appear in the diagonal of the chart.

Processes are divided into subsystems which correspond to major business functions, such as sales and management. Arrows are drawn between

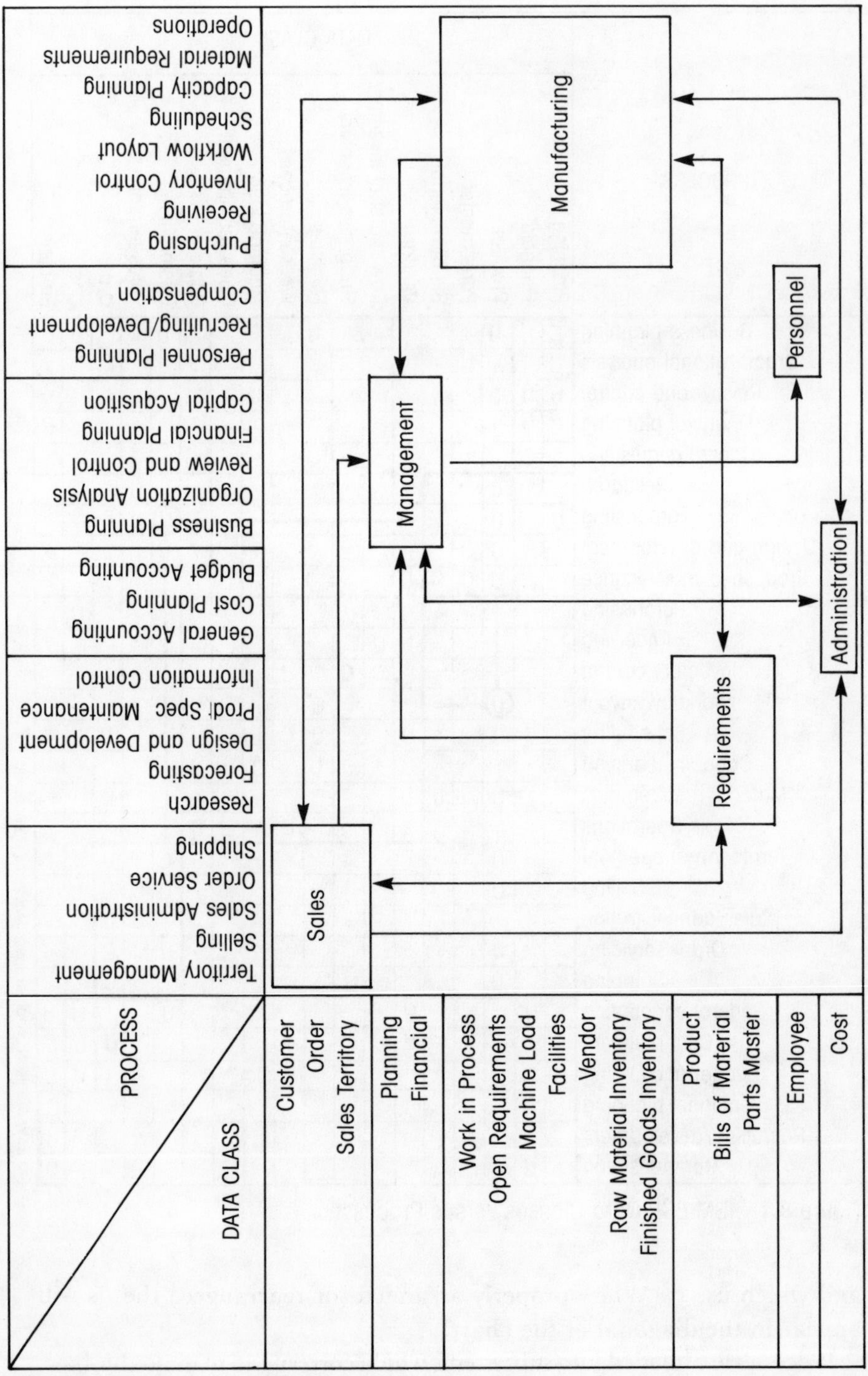

PROCESS / DATA CLASS

Processes:
- Territory Management
- Selling
- Sales Administration
- Order Service
- Shipping
- Research
- Forecasting
- Design and Development
- Prod: Spec: Maintenance
- Information Control
- General Accounting
- Cost Planning
- Budget Accounting
- Business Planning
- Organization Analysis
- Review and Control
- Financial Planning
- Capital Acquisition
- Personnel Planning
- Recruiting/Development
- Compensation
- Purchasing
- Receiving
- Inventory Control
- Workflow Layout
- Scheduling
- Capacity Planning
- Material Requirements
- Operations

Data Classes:
- Customer
- Order
- Sales Territory
- Planning
- Financial
- Work in Process
- Open Requirements
- Machine Load
- Facilities
- Vendor
- Raw Material Inventory
- Finished Goods Inventory
- Product
- Bills of Material
- Parts Master
- Employee
- Cost

Groupings: Sales, Requirements, Management, Manufacturing, Personnel, Administration

Figure 8.2 IBM BSP Subsystem Relationships

processes to indicate where data flow occurs. Finally, the diagram is rearranged for clarity and simplicity (see Figure 8.2). This is the Information Architecture.

Now the organization's required subsystems and the gaps between what's needed and what exists have been identified. Implementing the entire architecture will take several years. The major remaining short-term tasks are to determine architecture priorities, review information systems management and report. IBM recommends setting priorities according to four sets of criteria: potential benefits, impact on the organization, success factors and demand.

BSP has a number of significant strengths. It identifies data as a key corporate resource. It gets senior management involved. It provides a strong set of methodological tools for defining relationships between data and processes and among major systems. It enables an organization to identify gaps, redundancies and anomalies. It helps set priorities in designing traditional data processing system applications.

However, it also has a number of significant limitations. BSP is an expression of the time when the IBM host was the primary — and often the sole — repository of computer intelligence in the organization. It does not take into account the explosion of desktop computing, office technologies and user-driven activity. For these and perhaps other reasons, it has several weaknesses:

- Its concept of "top-down design, bottom-up implementation", while valid as an overall approach, fails to plan for the potential contributions of end-users in either the design or implementation phases. And while it is conceivable to keep end-users out of the "top-down" design phase, they now have tools to get into "bottom-up" implementation on their own.

- Although data classes are, quite properly, isolated from applications and processes for purposes of analysis, the separation is incomplete. Ultimately, BSP's version of Information Architecture does not follow through on this distinction. As will be seen in the next section, the distinction between "data" and "processes" is extremely important.

- A key related problem is that BSP does not give much help in the actual design of databases or in providing a detailed top-down view of their organization and contents. The data classes of BSP are similar to "subject" databases, with somewhat arbitrary categories.

- BSP reflects the traditional development cycle and centralized DP departments. Under this scenario, full implementation of the architecture (processes and data structures) depends on a system which is prey to specification problems, backlogs, poor productivity, and ongoing maintenance activity. Many DP departments are much too busy bailing out the boat to fix the leak using the same old methods.

- Although BSP makes a passing reference to non-automated information, there is no discussion of how this wealth of material — critical to most planning functions — fits in with Information Architecture.

James Martin:
Information Engineering

James Martin picks up where BSP ends. Martin's view is that computing technology is simply not being used as it should be. It is bogged down by huge backlogs (visible and invisible), productivity and maintenance problems. The most valuable potential benefit of computer power — the delivery of strategic information to management — is not being realized.[3]

At the same time, software tools are emerging which enable the end-user to seize control over the computer resource, in particular non-procedural fourth generation languages and query languages. Not only do these permit end-users to write many applications themselves. They also permit programmers to prototype applications for users before proceeding to full-scale development. Martin defines this as "user-driven programming".[4] He further identifies poor specifications as contributing to poor programs and suggests a variety of solutions, including the use of specification languages.

However, all these new techniques will be to no avail, he argues, unless the mess on the *data* side of data processing is cleaned up. In effect, the problem of data management is the critical barrier which is preventing the computer revolution from advancing. For this problem to be overcome, top management must address it and give full support to the data administration function.

The key design foundation, according to Martin, is the separation of data modeling from physical database design. Data should be structured according to its own internal logic, rather than on the basis of specific applications. Here, an *entity* is anything about which data can be stored — for example, a product, customer, salesman or part. The *data model* shows the relationships between entities. For example, a salesman is an employee and a branch office has many salesmen.

Entities have *attributes*; for example a salesman has a specific address, territory, quota, salary, and so on. The data model links attributes to entities.

Martin's view is that "Data have certain *inherent* properties which lead to correct structuring. These properties *are independent of how the data are used.*"[5]

Information engineering is the set of disciplines needed to build a computerized enterprise based on *data* systems. Its basic premises are that data lie at the center of modern data processing, and that the types of data used in an enterprise do not change very much. (Of course, the values of data change constantly.)

Martin proposes the following multi-phase planning methodology. (Note that the first two phases provide the foundation):

- *Strategic Information Planning* develops a business model, defining the objectives of the enterprise and what information is needed for it to accomplish its objectives.
- *Entity relationship analysis* is a top-down analysis of the types of data that must be kept and how they relate to one another.
- *Data modeling* creates the detailed, logical database design and attempts to make it as stable as possible before it is implemented. This can be structured into subject databases, using, for example, the Business Systems Planning matrix techniques discussed earlier.
- At this point end-users can gain access to the data with the aid of easy to use *query languages*.
- The data models are diagrammed, analyzed and used with data management systems to make them readily available for use with program applications.
- Fourth generation programming languages may be used for prototyping and design. Conventional third generation languages such as COBOL may also be used.

An Integrated Office Systems Perspective

BSP and James Martin's refinements provide effective approaches to constructing an information architecture for structured, computerized information which is internal to the organization. However, additional architectural requirements are posed by integrated office systems. Not all information related to decisionmaking in an electronic office environment is structured, computerized and resident in the organization. Figure 8.3 illustrates how the various sources of information are typically structured. A comprehensive architecture should take these into account.

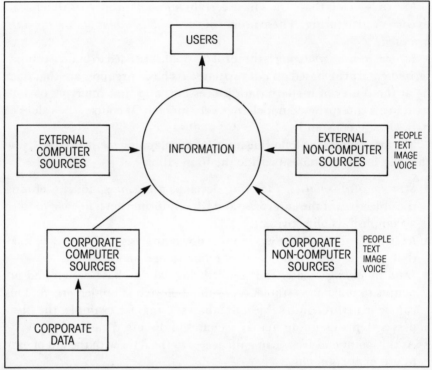

Figure 8.3   A Broader Perspective of Information

As shown in Figure 8.3, the information resource required by office personnel appears in many forms.

1. Corporate Computerized Data

The domain of most current approaches to information architecture is corporate data to be accessed, stored, manipulated and communicated through corporate computer facilities. Typically such data is resident on corporate mainframes and mini-computers, although there is a trend to factor the personal computer into the picture. These data are generally defined, managed and administered through the Data Processing department, or equivalent.

2. External Computer Sources

Publicly-available databases and services constitute a new category of computer-based information which must be included in the architecture. Sources include *databases* such as Dow Jones, Associated Press, bibliographic references, wage contract settlements, economic information, airline schedules, and others ranging from government information to hog prices. Literally thousands of such databases are easily accessible from almost anywhere. In addition there is a growing number of public computerized *services* which provide information that should be factored into the architecture. Two good examples are computer conferencing and electronic messaging systems. These services are provided by common carriers and others. In providing a communication vehicle to individuals outside the organization, such services can generate huge amounts of data.

Typically external databases are under the jurisdiction of the corporate library specialists. With the growth of personal computers, demand for such facilities has become more widespread. However, limited knowledge about the possible sources of information and inadequate training have inhibited the full use of such sources.

3. Corporate Non-Computerized Sources

Another component of the information architecture is information generated within the organization which is not in computer format. This includes paper files, microform, images such as photographs and drawings, and information acquired through internal voice communications such as tape recordings and dictation. Typically such information is managed (if at all) by a corporate records center or, in a distributed fashion, by departments or individuals across the organization. Included in this category is information which will not likely be in computerized form for some time to come, but which nevertheless is both critical to the organization's functioning and very much related to information which *is* computerized. Much of this information has traditionally been handled by records management methods.

Of small but growing significance in most organizations are "unstructured" text, image and voice files from various computer media. Typical examples are word processing documents, electronic mail, business graphics, computer-aided-design diagrams and voice messages. Although they are *created* and *stored* electronically, such files are typically *managed via traditional records management* techniques. With improvements in management techniques and growth of this information base itself, large portions of the "unstructured" information base will shift to the computer.

One major source of information which is generally overlooked in systematic design efforts is people. It is generally assumed that we can get hold of the individuals who can answer our questions through our personal or formal networks. However, this produces the best results only under the right conditions. Generally, organizations do not take advantage of the knowledge their own employees have. For example, very few companies systematically "debrief" — or even use as a reference source — all people who have joined the company from competitive organizations.

4. External Non-Computer Sources
Various types of information which are not computerized and which origi-
nate outside the organization also form part of the picture. Examples are
magazine articles, television programs, films, videotapes and discs, research reports, external correspondence, product announcements, press
releases, seminar and course advertisements, external meetings and telephone calls. The planning for and use of such information, even though
it might be strategic or critical in nature, is often handled in a decentralized, ad hoc fashion.

All this information together constitutes the information resource. A comprehensive approach to Information Architecture should include a strategy to define, plan for, oversee the acquisition of, structure and manage
that information from those sources which are strategic or which have
corporate-wide implications.

This is by no means an argument to centralize the management of all
information within the organization, or to do for all information what
data processing does for computerized information. Rather, it is a case
for reviewing the strategic or corporate-wide information requirements
of the organization, as part of the strategic planning process for integrated office systems. Therefore a more comprehensive review or modeling process can lead to an architecture for this information that will enable its capture, management and access to appropriate users for critical
decisionmaking activities. Such a broader view of the problem also requires some new approaches to implementing an Information Architecture.

Information Modeling

A comprehensive approach geared to the needs of the integrated office
will include *all information sources* in the model. The product of this
effort will be used primarily to support planning, design and decisionmaking by executives, managers and professionals. This contrasts to the
data-driven architecture, whose primary function is to support operational processes, with management information as an important, but secondary byproduct.

This difference in function means that the design of a comprehensive
information architecture must be user driven. A new approach is required.
The basis of the new approach is information modeling based on an Information Requirements Assessment. Its purpose is to define, within a
structured framework, the multiple information requirements of various
levels within the organization.

The assessment should begin with the needs of senior management and key individuals responsible for planning in various departments. It should then move through a sample of individuals across the organization from every function, and at each level.

The Information Requirements Assessment is based on a four-step approach, including: 1) User Requirements Survey, 2) Information Source/Resource Analysis, 3) Information Distribution Analysis, and 4) an optional Information Process Flow Analysis.

Based on the results of the survey, appropriate organizational structures, policies and procedures and alternative implementation approaches can be developed. This will ensure that strategic information can be made available in a timely manner to people who need it.

User Requirements Survey

A detailed picture of information needs can be developed through the use of structured interviews based on an interview guide and questionnaire. The following categories of questions will need to be answered in regard to each information topic. (As an illustration, some typical information needs of a marketing manager are provided in parentheses):

- **User** (Marketing Manager): function level, responsibilities (sales, sales management, vertical markets)
- **Topic** and **issue** classifications: primary classification (marketing), secondary classifications (product, competitive, market opportunities)
- **Business uses** (forecasting, vertical market strategies, product requirements planning)
- **Use** (view/print, view/analyze, print), integrate (multiple media), merge with other data, etc.
- **Sources**: specific (e.g., internal/external databases by name, publications, reports, files), general (libraries, research sources, consultants)
- **Format**: structure (text, table, layout, key issues), media (human source, paper, computer file)
- **Critical factors**: urgency, frequency, retention, and security/access.

The results of this survey are subjected to qualitative and quantitative analysis. Various elements are mapped against each other in matrix fashion to provide a graphic representation of how current needs are being met. Gaps in meeting user needs are identified. One result of this survey will be the uncovering of new "leads" for information sources which might be of value to other people.

It should be noted that this survey will be enriched if design input is provided by experts in fields such as current corporate databases and corporate records management. Well-informed subject matter experts and bibliographic experts may also be of help.

Information Source/Resource Analysis

The next major phase is to map user information requirements against location information. Both internal and external sources should be included. A view of the span of the information map is depicted in Figure 8.4.

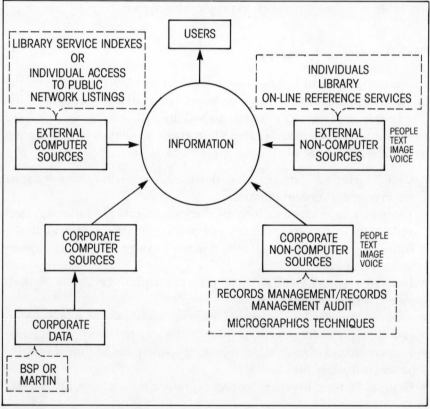

Figure 8.4   Types of Information

Where structured data is part of the information requirement, tools such as IBM's Business Systems Planning can be used to relate data classes to information requirements. It is possible to take this exercise to the data element level, if required.

Similarly, for corporate non-computer sources, Records Management audit techniques may be used to uncover the various locations of required information. Records Management may also be used to build a coherent classification scheme, if one does not already exist.

In addition to providing a directory of information resources, an evaluation component may be included in this phase. For example, a large brewing company used the chart depicted in Figure 8.5 to provide information about how well various sources meet the desired usage requirements.

Information Distribution Analysis

If the current state of information delivery is accepted as the most efficient manner in which to serve the needs of the users, then there will not be a great deal to change. However, there are likely many opportunities to enhance the delivery, and improve on the utility of information delivered to users. For example, a monthly sales report delivered via a manually prepared paper report may contain the information required. However, it might be more useful if the information were available on an "on-demand" basis, and if some forecasting analysis could take place using decision support tools. This requires that the information be available in an online system.

Therefore, the Information Distribution Analysis should identify *the gaps between availability and need*. The media or format, timing, sources, even content could change once this mapping has taken place.

Information Process Flow Analysis

Information flowcharting will help with understanding the relationships between activities, people who perform them, the information used at each step and the amount of time between activities where information is inactive, or "floating", in order to fully understand the degree to which changes are required. Sometimes forms are used to pass along information. Quite frequently, a very convoluted and inefficient process has evolved around the movement of this information. The potential may exist to streamline the flow of form-based information and to provide access to the information via an electronic forms handler or database.

The Use of Information Models

Models are sometimes helpful in understanding the relationship of process to information inputs and products. A model of interaction and information use can clarify the alternative approaches to implementation.

	A	B	C	D	E	F	G	H	I	J	TOT
1.		1	2				2			0	5
2.	1		2							0	3
3.	3	1		5			2			0	11
4.		1		5			2			0	8
5.										0	
6.										0	
7.					5	5		5	5	0	20
TOT	4	3	4	10	5	5	6	5	5	0	

1
2
3
4
5

} On a scale from 1 to 5 measures the effectiveness with which a particular source covers the issue/content identified.

1   ineffective
5   highly effective

o — activity covers, no ranking
x — activity not covered

PRODUCTS

Contents

1. Aluminum Cans/Returnable Bottles
2. Distribution Analyses
3. Product Research and Development
4. Packaging Analyses
5. Product Summaries and Variances
6. Productivity Analyses
7. Regulations (governing production packaging and distribution)

Sources

A — Association Reports
B — Industry Publications
C — Industry Warehousing Reports
D — Consultants' Reports (external)
E — Department of Consumer and Corporate Affairs (Federal)
F — Department of National Health and Welfare (Federal)
G — FOODS/ADLIBRA (electronic bibliographic database)
H — Marketing Agency (Provincial)
I — Ministries of Consumer and Commercial Relations (Provincial)
J — Other (internal sources)

Figure 8.5   External Computer Source Evaluation

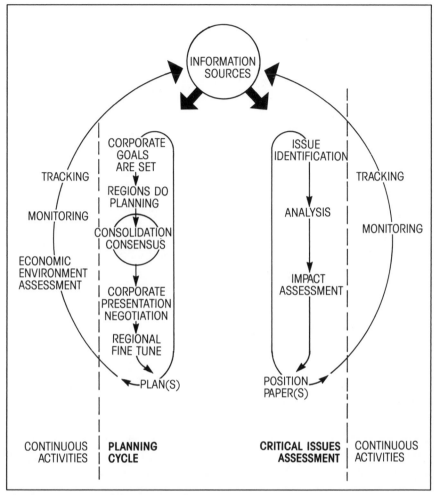

Figure 8.6   Interaction Between Processes

Figure 8.6 indicates the relationship between the strategic business planning and critical issues management processes within the brewing company mentioned earlier. This model led us to conclude that the "information resource" was the critical component in improving two key business processes, and that the processes are highly dependent upon each other. Before the study, the two major processes — planning and critical issues assessment — were completely separate. Information sources were not managed systematically (see Figure 8.7), and very little information passed between the two major processes.

The implementation approach was based upon the steps and models described in the previous sections. It became apparent that lack of access

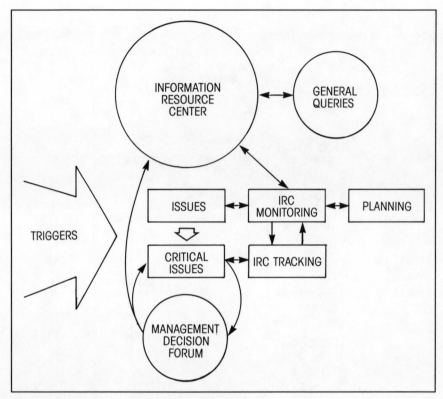

Figure 8.7 Information Management Model

to paper-based records, external databases for environment scanning, and other sources of electronic and paper-based information was impeding the organization's ability to manage issues in a proactive manner.

Implementation: The Information Resource Center

In the previous example, the concept of an Information Resource Center (IRC) was planned as a first step towards ensuring that all required information would be available at a corporate level. The Information Resource Center (see Figure 8.8) is a new organizational form designed to help meet the information requirements of the electronic office.

The IRC is the central reference point for the full range of strategic information needs in the organization. Given that it is currently impractical to transform all information into a single consistent electronic format for online access, an interim approach is to develop an online index to all information resources identified. Pointers are used to indicate the location of the information, be it external or internal.

To access external, and some internal, databases, it is too time-consuming, costly and inefficient to train every user in each database access method and query language the same applies to paper filing systems. So, a trained Information Resource Center Specialist helps locate information.

Services range from general query (reactive), through selective dissemination (proactive), which is based on user interest profiles. The IRC

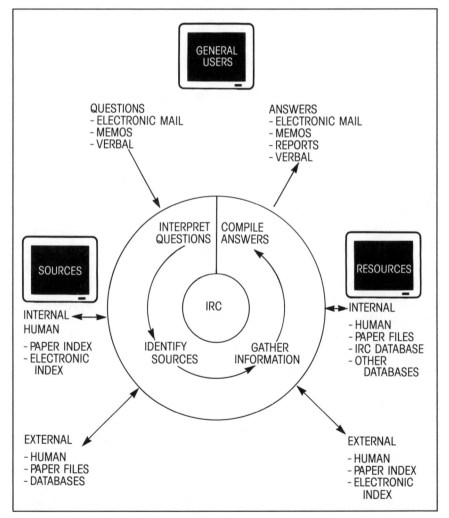

Figure 8.8   Information Resource Center

is also the logical center for records management coordination, library services, orientation and education/training for the service itself.

It is necessary to have a structured model of the existing information resources and requirements before they can be managed, and appropriate access provided. Once this has been done, the IRC can be piloted in one location to serve the needs of a common user-level group whose needs can be met with the current information base. This does not preclude individuals, workgroups, departments and others maintaining databases of information, but rather identifies that a particular database exists and provides the user with an indication of where to locate it.

The decision on whether to centralize or decentralize the IRC can be based on the information map that indicates how much of the information resource is commonly needed. If large volumes of information are unique to specific groups, a decentralized approach might be more effective.

The IRC should not be confused with the Information Center — an organizational concept popularized by IBM during the late 1970s. The Information Center helps end-users develop data processing applications, learn to program in very powerful high-level languages, use personal computers and gain access to existing host-based databases. However, a natural progression is to combine the IRC and the Information Center functions. In this way, the traditional Information Center is expanded to include all forms of information, rather than just structured data.

A second key scenario is the role of the IRC as part of an issues management system. Here the IRC goes beyond providing routine information tailored to individual need. The IRC now takes on the more dynamic tasks of issue monitoring and tracking. As an issue moves through its cycle, information needs change; the IRC responds to these changing needs by continually adjusting its sources and reference materials.

Other future scenarios could include information monitoring to feed into an Issues Management System, Issues Conferences using computer conferencing tools, electronic bulletin board and general corporate communications functions. As the technology evolves and query arbitration systems using natural language techniques become viable, there will be less need for an information technician to conduct the index and database searches and more opportunities for the individual user to interact directly with the system.

Communications Architecture for Open Systems

The purpose of any computer network is to provide access paths between end-users or devices at different locations. Traditional computer networks tended to be "closed systems". That is, they were self-contained systems for one function or organization and typically enabled communication only between devices of a single vendor. However, by the late seventies technology developments had started to change this picture and a need for a new approach to networks began to be evident.

The general proliferation of intelligent devices such as word processors, personal computers, display telephones, intelligent copiers, and other computing or computer-related devices has been matched by an equal proliferation of "high tech" vendors.

As a result of these developments, the question being posed in more and more organizations is: "How can we develop a strategy that can enable these various tools and devices to communicate with each other and with the outside world?"

Any vendor who plans to keep pace with the convergence in telecommunications, computer and office technologies must address that question in terms of its product portfolio and strategy. Likewise, a coherent answer is fundamental to building a successful technology strategy in user organizations, so let's begin.

There are many ways of characterizing communications networks.

1. Geography
Some networks are constructed to enable communication within a restricted geographical area such as a building. Other networks are designed to enable access across a wider geographical area. These are usually referred to as *local area networks* and *wide area networks* respectively.

2. Public or Private
Private links can be leased from a common carrier (an organization authorized and regulated by the Federal Communications Commission in

the U.S. and by the Canadian Radio-television and Telecommunications Commission in Canada) or from the postal, telephone and telegraph (PTT) authority in most other countries. As well, these carriers provide "public" access to shared networks on a pay-as-you-go basis. To complicate matters, "closed user groups" may be established in public networks to provide the appearance of a dedicated network.

3. Switched or Dedicated

Networks which provide variable communications paths among a group of subscribers are called switched communications networks. One example is the telephone network. Networks which provide a continuous communication path between specific subscribers are called non-switched. Examples are the radio and television broadcasting networks, microwave networks and some timesharing networks.

4. Services Provided or Application

Networks can be categorized according to the capabilities they deliver. For example there are banking networks, airline networks, and cable television networks.

5. Topology

Networks can have different topological structures which outline the arrangement of the transmission paths and nodes of the network. These include the star, ring, tree, bus, multi-drop, and mesh. A network has both a physical and logical structure which need not be identical. (Note that these terms will all be discussed later in this chapter.)

6. Vendor

Many of the major computer manufacturers have developed their own networking software, which can also serve to differentiate networks. It is not uncommon, for example, to hear a discussion of IBM's SNA network.

While there are numerous other ways of categorizing networks, the most commonly used groupings with office systems will likely be into local and wide area networks. Before discussing the reasons for this and the issues of network strategy in these two areas it is important to explain the concept of network protocols and, in particular, use of the International Standards Organization's reference model (ISO 7498-1983) for comparing networks. The discussion of these topics in the following sections has been kept as non-technical as possible, delving into only enough detail to enable the senior executive to formulate a high-level strategy for communication compatibility and evolution.

Network Protocols and the OSI Reference Model

A communications *architecture* is an overall structure, or blueprint, for a corporate communications system, which includes a network architecture — that is, a number of individual *protocols*. A protocol is a set of rules and procedures for the network which defines how two or more devices interact to transfer information — for example, how information on the network is to be formatted and what commands and responses are to be used in the exchange of messages. In network terminology, an *implementation* is a running version of the architecture, or blueprint. The development of this architecture is central to any network strategy for integrated systems as is providing a mechanism for it to evolve over time as needs change and technology advances.

Overcoming the "incompatibility" of various office devices has become a central theme of office automation in the eighties. Indeed, a good case could be made that "incompatibilitaphobia" — deep seated dread of incompatability — has swept the land. (Note that typical symptoms include a morbid fear of making major capital expenditures in the area of office systems, a burning desire to tie-up vendor marketing representatives in coaxial cable, and impulsive urges to chuck microcomputers out the windows of tall office towers.)

How have we arrived at such a sad state of affairs? Traditional voice communication networks had limited functions — such as dialing and transmission and error control. With computer communications, other issues such as variability of speed, format and access procedures — all of which can be unique to each device — became important.

For years there was no cross-vendor standardization of protocols for computer networks, so user organizations attempted to grapple with the problem in ways which were generally unsatisfactory. Single vendor approaches were restrictive and appropriate only as long as single vendor environments existed. The development of unique protocols within an organization was usually a costly dead end. Others tried to adapt widely used protocols to their own situation. With the advent of integrated office systems, which use general applications for a large number of users, this challenge has become very significant.

A network architecture must therefore define the access paths, procedures and rules which enable devices and people not only to be *connected* to each other, but also to actually *communicate*. The distinction between the two words is important. It is of little value to a user to have his or her workstation connected to another computer, if only a meaningless stream of bits is exchanged. An often used analogy is that it doesn't do you much good to place a long distance telephone call to Japan if you only speak English and the person at the other end only speaks Japanese.

To address this problem in the industry, various standards bodies are working to adopt standard protocols. These include the ISO and the CCITT, (Consultative Committee for International Telephone and Telegraph), which is a consortium of PTT, common carrier organizations and many national bodies (such as the National Bureau of Standards in the U.S.). CCITT, for example, adopted the widely used X.25 access method for packet-switched networks. The Institute of Electrical and Electronics Engineers (IEEE) has taken the lead in defining standards for local area networks. The International Standards Organization developed the protocol for data link control called HDLC. Much work is going on to provide standards for document and message communications (for example, Message Handling Systems Protocol from CCITT, MOTIS from ISO).

The Reference Model of Open Systems Interconnection

Probably the most important effort, from the standpoint of strategic network planning for office systems in user organizations, is the International Standards Organization's Reference Model for Open Systems Interconnection (OSI). This was accepted as a world standard in 1983. The model specifies a seven-layer architecture for the exchange of information among open systems. Work is continuing in the ISO and its member bodies (such as the American National Standards Institute and the Canadian Standards Association) to define protocols for each of the layers, including protocols for messaging, file transfer, and document interchange. *Because the ISO's OSI model is a reference point for much of the other standardization work underway, as well as the foundation for building a network architecture of integrated systems, it is important for senior managers and planners to understand it.*

The term "open system" refers to the ability of equipment from different vendors to both connect and communicate through telecommunications media. The OSI model consists of seven layers that divide the communications process into sets of related services. Each layer is based on services provided by lower layers and provides services for higher layers in the model. The layers are strictly separated so that one layer can be changed or improved without affecting the others. Figure 9.1 illustrates the OSI model, whose seven layers will be explained in detail. Note that the OSI model is a *reference model* defining the different layers of services a network can provide. It does not itself contain the actual *protocols* or standards. Rather, it provides a structure for such standard activities. Understanding the concept of layers is important for understanding the issue of

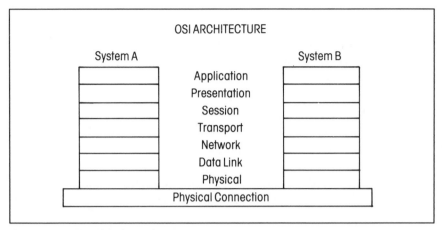

Figure 9.1   The ISO Open Systems Interconnection Model

compatibility. We don't suggest mastery of the model; an overview will do for most senior planners.

1. The Physical Layer
The lowest layer of the OSI model defines services for the transmission of bits (the basic unit of data) and the control of circuits. This includes making a physical connection and providing the electrical, functional and procedural characteristics to establish, maintain and release physical connections.

2. Data Link Layer
The second layer governs the operation of an individual link, and regulates things such as error detection and correction. One example of a data link protocol is HDLC, also developed by the International Standards Organization.

3. The Network Layer
This layer regulates the routing and switching of packets from one network node to another, regardless of whether these nodes exist on the same or different networks.

4. Transport Layer
The transport layer governs the end-to-end (by computer-to-computer) transportation of messages, and masks the service user from all variations in network type or quality. The Transport Service provides an effective "highway" for user messages to travel, and ensures that the messages are delivered regardless of "road" conditions.

5. The Session Layer

A session defines a period of activity between two higher level entities. The session layer regulates the binding and unbinding of these entities as well as the control of the dialogue between them for exchange, synchronization and delimiting of data.

6. The Presentation Layer

This layer provides a set of services that may be selected by the highest layer (application layer) to enable it to interpret the meaning of the data exchanged. These services relate to what is often referred to as the syntax of the messages. In the example of a telephone call to Japan cited earlier, the presentation layer provides the choice of English or Japanese words.

7. The Application Layer

The highest layer of the OSI model provides protocols to directly serve user-specific computer applications such as electronic mail, communication of graphics and access to databases. If nodes such as computers or terminals are compatible at the applications layer, then text documents, for example, communicated between two nodes with similar text-processing capabilities on the network would have the same meaning at either end of the communication.

It should be noted here that even if devices are both using the same protocols, even at the highest layer, this does not mean that what you get at one end is *identical* to what you get at the other. For example, a document containing sophisticated graphics, boldface type, and scientific notation which is sent to a micro with more modest capabilities, will obviously not appear the same as when it was on the more powerful computer. In this case a "lowest common denominator" would have to be negotiated in which those characters and codes which the receiving station could not understand were avoided. The goal (of course) is to ensure a common understanding between the parties (semantic equivalence).

The model helps you clarify and understand the morass of various networks and standards which exist today. For example, the lower three layers of the OSI model correspond approximately to CCITT X.25 standard for packet-switched networks which is now widely implemented. As a result protocols at these levels are well-defined and effectively adopted. However, protocols at the higher levels are more complex. As well, many competing vendors of computer systems have proprietary protocols at the higher levels, so there are many raging debates, both within and outside the standards bodies, regarding which approaches are best.

Consider IBM's System Network Architecture, which describes the rules

for network design, management and application development in the
IBM environment. SNA was designed before the OSI model was adopted.
Although it is difficult to precisely "map" SNA functions against the layers of
OSI, the two are roughly equivalent, with SNA stopping short of the sev-
enth OSI layer. In many organizations, SNA is the de facto networking
standard. DIA (Document Interchange Architecture) and DCA (Document
Content Architecture) are higher level protocols designed to "top off"
SNA. IBM has been developing gateways between its products and ISO
standards such as X.25. Many other vendors, such as Digital Equipment
Corporation and Wang, have made an effort to use OSI rules to help define their own networking products.

A variety of useful end-user products are beginning to emerge under
the OSI umbrella. For example, teletex provides for the exchange of formatted documents between word processors and includes access to world-
wide telex and future facsimile capabilities. The Message Handling System protocol developed by the CCITT is designed to permit the exchange
of information in any medium (text, data, voice or facsimile) among various public networks and between public and private networks. Because it
includes an interpersonal messaging service, messaging may become as
widespread as the voice telephone network. The North American Presentation Level Protocol Syntax (NAPLPS) is an international sixth-level standard for videotex computer graphics communication, based on Canadian-
developed Telidon.

A key emerging direction is the Integrated Services Digital Network
(ISDN). The telephone companies are switching over to fully digital
networks, so that even voice conversations will be carried as a series of
bits rather than the traditional analog pattern. The same technology will
be used to handle data and image information for a truly integrated service.

The OSI model can provide a basis for developing an overall network
strategy and a model for understanding the current networks in your
organization. It clearly provides a policy framework for network planning for the present and the future. Any technology strategy should include a corporate policy that networks must utilize standards that con-
form to the OSI model. In the shorter term, a transition plan that provides
for evolution to protocol standards, especially for higher layers, should
be developed.

Local Area Networks

With an understanding of the OSI model we are in a better position to
discuss the topic of local area networks and integrate a plan for LANs into
the overall network strategy.

As mentioned at the beginning of the chapter, traditional networks have been serving "local" offices for years. Computer networks enabled various terminals, printers and other peripherals to connect to a central computer. A second type of local network has been the telephone network, in which telephones in an office are all attached to a private branch exchange (PBX).

However, all such traditional local networks had a couple of noteworthy features. They all attached various peripheral devices to a central hub and they were typically single-vendor or plug compatible. With the movement towards desktop computing we have seen the rise of a new generation of networks — so different from previous local networks that they have acquired exclusive rights to the term "local area networks".

The term became popular at the end of the 1970s with the announcement by Xerox of Ethernet, primarily the child of the company's Palo Alto Research Center. Realizing that the photocopier business would change in the move towards the "paperless office" and appreciating the huge market opportunities provided by integrated office systems, Xerox launched a number of office systems products, including a word processor and a microcomputer. However, as it entered into these new markets it needed a network strategy which would enable its products to work together.

The Xerox strategists judged that the only way they could compete with the major computer manufacturers, as well as its office products competitors, was to develop a network strategy which they would publish and attempt to have adopted as a standard. Xerox teamed up with DEC and the chip manufacturer Intel and announced the Ethernet standard for local area networks. Subsequently, the designs have been submitted to the IEEE 802 committee for standardization. The Ethernet architecture addresses the lower two layers of the OSI model. With the announcement of Ethernet, a flurry of interest and debate on the topic was precipitated. Today more and more users are moving towards a LAN approach even though the road is often circuitous, rocky and complex.

LANs based on industry-wide standards can enable integration in the office through interconnecting terminals, computers and other devices for the exchange and sharing of information. They also permit orderly incremental growth and evolution of systems and provide the potential to interconnect equipment from different vendors.

Another side of the case for LANs is that they can save money, including the often huge costs of wiring every device directly to a central hub (which can be huge). Overall systems costs are reduced through resource sharing, as are the costs of connecting new devices as interconnection is simplified.

Clearly, LANs *do* a lot of things. But what exactly *is* a local area network? There are many different definitions. The IEEE 802 Committee (a key international body adopting standards for LANs) defines a LAN as:

> A data communications system which allows a number of independent data devices to communicate with each other ... confined to a moderate sized geographical area ... and a moderate data rate ... in contrast to long distance networks ..., networks which interconnect equipment inside one room, or networks of devices inside one piece of equipment. (LANS are) ... intended to allow distributed data processing and hardware and resource sharing between equipment using the network. The applications environment for a local network is intended to be commercial and light industrial.[1]

The new LANs have a number of common features that help clarify and define them. In general, a LAN is a network for communication:

- among nodes such as computers, terminals and other devices;
- within a relatively restricted geographical area;
- usually owned by one organization;
- usually for digital communications, but eventually also for analog (such as full video);
- which should be open — that is, any vendor can supply nodes for the network if they adopt the public protocols of that network; and
- should be transparent (i.e., the user can communicate over the network, as with a dumb telephone, without knowing how the network works).

There are now close to two hundred vendors in the LAN market. Most are either computer/office system vendors, PBX vendors, or specialized LAN vendors. To sort through the technology of this LAN jungle it is also important to understand the three key technical dimentions of the topic: 1) topology, 2) transmission medium, and 3) multiplexing and access method.

The LAN **topology** refers to the physical and logical configuration of the network. There are a number of topologies, the main ones being the bus, ring, star and hybrid networks. These are illustrated in Figure 9.2.

While each topology has certain advantages and disadvantages there is no one "best" topology in the short run (although in the long run, *hybrid* configurations may make the most sense). The topology adopted should be shaped largely by organizational requirements and the organization's current technological base.

While the topology selected determines many network issues, it is largely independent of the choice of **transmission medium**.

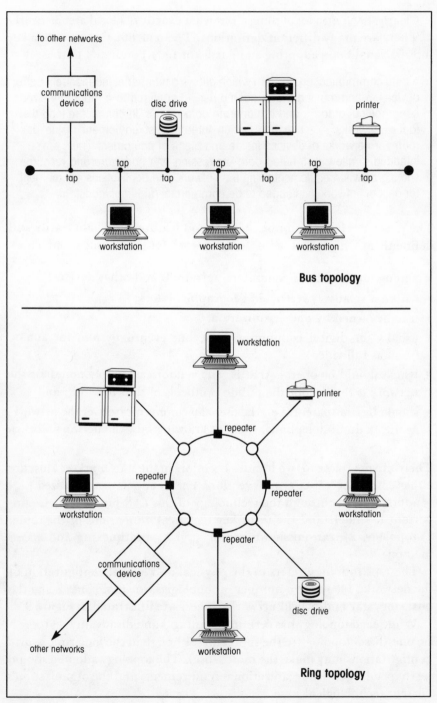

Figure 9.2 LAN Topologies

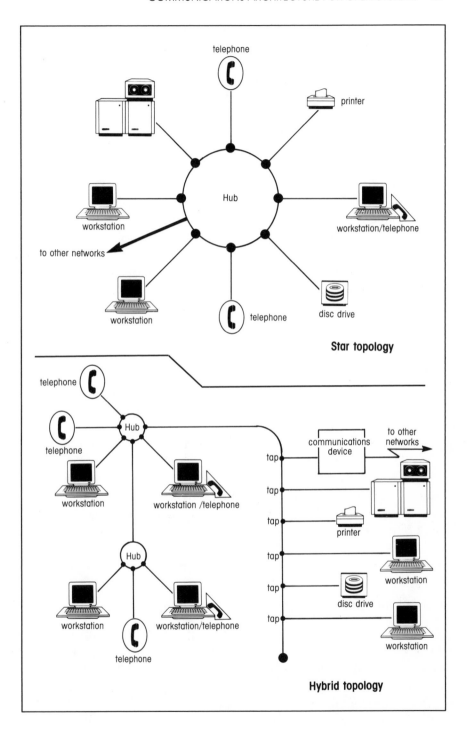

Star topology

Hybrid topology

Twisted pair wires used for telephones have the advantage of omni-presence. Virtually every building in the western world is wired for telephone wire. If this can be used as the main transmission medium for the local network there can be huge savings in costs and resources for network installation and growth. Current developments are significantly improving the capacity of twisted wires.

Coaxial cable (baseband or broadband) has the main advantage of high capacity. Baseband transmission is digital and the normal maximum distance for the network is two kilometres. Broadband wire is divided into different analog frequency bands using radio frequency (RF) modems. The maximum distance can be longer than with baseband. It is also possible to have a "baseband band" within a broadband network.

Fiber optics will probably become an increasingly important transmission medium. Such a cable has a number of advantages: very high bandwidth, small size, light weight, superior immunity to electromagnetic interference, and good security.

Other media which are beginning to appear include radio transmission for broadcasting information and infrared light for point-to-point communications (such as between close buildings). Additionally, hybrid networks that utilize more than one form of media are possible.

Finally, the various transmission media will require different techniques for the devices sharing them to gain **access and multiplex** information onto the network. There are two basic multiplexing techniques — time division multiplexing (TDM) and frequency division multiplexing (FDM).

There are various combinations of topology, transmission medium, multiplexing and access method on the market, but there is no one "best" LAN. It is not possible to sort through this complex technical web independently of the user requirements and needs of the organization. Rather, the best approach will depend on what the organization wants the network to do both now and in the future.

This means that a network strategy must be part of the overall process of strategic planning for integrated office systems.

Role of the PBX

Another key issue in the process of planning is the relationship of the PBX to the overall network strategy. This concrete issue is central to the broader issue of how data, voice, text and image will be used in the office and how they should be integrated.

Most of the main PBX vendors are positioning their products to enter the LAN wars. The attack seems to have two main phases. The first phase saw the digital PBX providing the capability to switch data as well as voice. This capability became available in the early 1980s, from vendors such as Northern Telecom (SL 100, SL 1); Mitel (SX 2000); Rolm (CBX); Intecom (IBX), and Lexar (LBX).

Used in this limited fashion, the PBX can provide a natural, low-risk bridge to office networking. If data and voice are multiplexed together on twisted pair wires, the bandwidth is adequate for most workstation requirements. There are a some limitations to this approach, however. The additional load could overburden existing telephone circuits. The network is also vulnerable to catastrophic failure because of total reliance on the PBX. As well, there may be problems handling some computer-to-computer communications, image transfer and video, because of the bandwidth limitations of twisted pair wire.

The second phase of PBX approaches to local area networks was announced by many of the leading vendors in 1983. In this, the PBX star topology is integrated with other types of local networks such as Ethernet, as in the example depicted in Figure 9.3.

In this scenario, the PBX is central to the complete LAN. The facilities that can be attached to this PBX include:

- Telephones containing an Add-on Data Module (ADM) or other capability enabling a computer terminal or intelligent workstation to connect to the PBX through the telephone.
- Microcomputers with attached peripherals.
- Computer terminals with limited local intelligence.
- Display telephones. In Figure 9.3 there are two telephone lines going to the switch (one for voice and one for data).
- Coaxial cable LAN(s). An example would be a network like Ethernet. Various devices are attached to the Ethernet, including communications processors which could provide access to other facilities, such as the company mainframe.

Using such an approach any user could have access to any device that was permitted. Whether an individual user is connected to the network directly through the PBX or through the Ethernet depends on the individual requirements (for example, computer-to-computer communications may require coaxial cable). So all the benefits of resource sharing, easy growth, and cost savings that LANs are designed to deliver should be achieved. Note that such a scenario would be limited to organizations which have strong requirements to deliver analog information, such as full video, to each workstation.

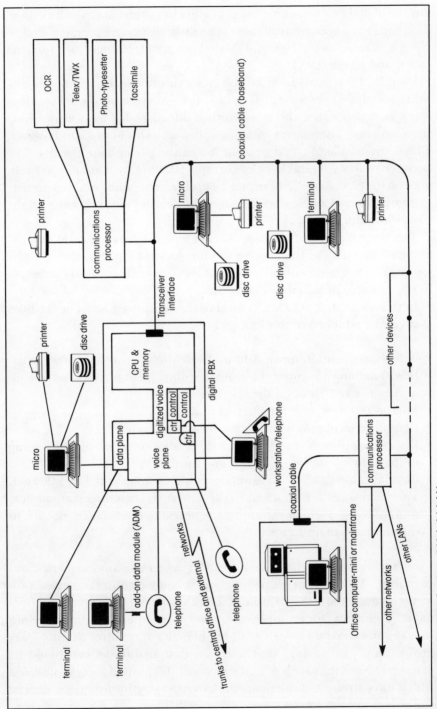

Figure 9.3 A PBX-Centered Hybrid LAN

Obviously, the PBX can be an important part of the LAN picture and should not be ignored in the development of office communications strategies.

Wide Area Networks

The second part of an overall network strategy is the plan for wide area networks. Networks which go beyond a single location have always been critical, even for organizations located in one building. These networks enable:

- Communication among disparate parts of an organization
- Resource-sharing across geographical locations
- Access to information across the organization, as appropriate
- Construction of distributed databases to improve many aspects of data resource management
- Access to the growing number of publicly available databases.

There are a number of different approaches to building a strategy for wide area communications beyond the bounds of a local area network. There is a considerable body of knowledge and literature on this topic already, and it is not necessary to repeat this information here. However, it is useful to point to several overall trends in network strategy.

Trends in Network Architectures

TREND: Network planning is becoming more important
The implementation of multifunction and multi-media workstations for potentially all personnel in an enterprise has obvious implications for the amount of effort that will have to go into network planning. Increasingly, the office is becoming a system rather than a place. More and more people can work independently using advanced workstation tools. Possible locations include remote offices, customer locations, at home or, for that matter, on the beach. To do this, the networks required will be vastly more complex. Since the workstation on the desktop must communicate with other persons and facilities, both within and external to the organization, planning a network becomes a more critical and complex challenge. As a result there is a trend to treat a network as a system which has users, resources and other requirements, just like a traditional data processing system.

It is also important to note that network costs are becoming a greater proportion of overall system costs. Unlike costs for computers, especially micros, which have fallen or remained constant with skyrocketing gains in capability, network costs have, in general, increased. One of the problems is that many network components (for example wire) are not subject to the cost reductions of the chip in the same way as computers are. Another is that network requirements grow exponentially as the number of users increases.

TREND: Towards standard protocols for open systems
The multi-vendor environment has become a fact of life for virtually all organizations. Typically the telephone system is provided by one supplier. Often there is more than one mini-computer or mainframe supplier. Usually there is more than one supplier of personal computers, word processors, printers, and similar equipment. In order to move from closed, single-vendor systems to open systems, more and more standard protocols are being used.

As explained earlier, the reference model for understanding the issue of compatibility is the ISO's Open Systems Interconnection model. However, within that framework, there is also a clear trend towards the use of standardized protocols at each layer of the model, rather than organizations attempting to build their own proprietary protocols, as has often been done in the past (see Figure 9.4).

This view is generally accepted in regard to the lower layers of the OSI model. Few would attempt to build their own version of the lower layer HDLC protocol, for example. However, at the higher layers, we still see many organizations constructing specialized protocols. For example, many companies have built proprietary protocols for text messaging systems that govern higher layer issues (such as the format for presenting the message on the screen). Rather than taking this approach, it is wiser to acquire a package or construct a system which corresponds to formal standards such as those being developed for Messaging Handling Systems and/or *de facto* standards such as the Document Interchange Architecture (DIA) and Document Content Architecture (DCA) being advanced by IBM. Another example is the use of the North American Presentation Level Protocol Standard (NAPLPS) for the presentation of business graphics and public information.

TREND: The rise of digital networks
The wide area telephone network is rapidly being converted from an analog system to digital as various analog central office switches are replaced

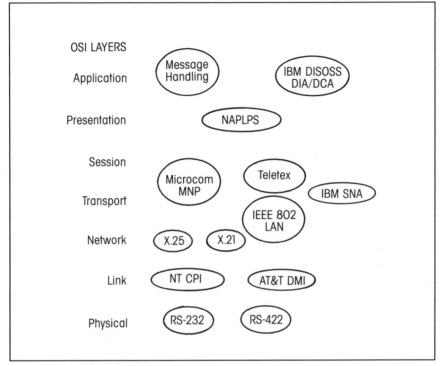

Figure 9.4   Standards and the OSI Reference Model

with digital switches. This trend is also occurring within organizations and buildings as analog PBXs and key sets are replaced with their digital counterparts. The implications of a fully digital network are profound for network planning. We are seeing the rise of the compound document — where data, text, voice and image can be stored and transmitted as a unified whole. The need for expensive modems, or modulation/demodulation equipment, to convert between analog and digital will be reduced.

TREND: The problem of security is growing
The implied downside of "open systems" is their potential for a huge security problem. The interconnection of various resources and people across the organization and outside it poses the problem of unauthorized or inappropriate access of system facilities. The problem is enhanced sharply by the increased use of public networks which may expose your organization's systems to criminals, competitors and kids. If cost is not a consideration, systems can be made extremely secure. However, given that cost is usually a factor, the issue of planning for secure systems becomes an issue of risk management. That is, what tradeoff between the

risk of system violation on the one hand and cost on the other is acceptable?

There are security issues at every layer of the OSI model. For example, at the physical or Data Link layers, the issue is: "Is there anyone listening in on the wire?" The Network layer poses the question of consistent security across the network, raising issues such as: "What happens with encrypted information when we link two networks together?" The Transport and Session layers address issues such as making sure the right person gets the right document. The Applications layer deals with issues such as individual identifiers and passwords, and access to files, directories or tools on the system.

The trend towards more complex security issues means that more attention will have to be applied to defining security requirements; to assessing and weighing the risks of various security tradeoffs; and to planning a network architecture which can ensure appropriate security at all layers of the model.

TREND: Increased use of public networks

Traditional wide area networks drew heavily on the use of private lines. Such circuits were leased from common carriers and were often used for large volume batch-oriented computer communications within the organization. Several things are changing this picture. One is the growing requirement for communications between enterprises and between traveling or remote individuals and their base office. A second is the growth of value-added networks which provide a host of computing services ranging from Dow Jones listings to airline schedules. A third is the widespread implementation of public packet-switched networks, which separate information into packets which can be interspersed with the packets of other users on the same wire. Packet-switching optimizes the use of the wire through sharing, resulting in lower costs.

Consequently one part of a network plan will be a strategy to take advantage of these new public networks.

TREND: Growing importance of network management

The growing importance, complexity and use of networks makes it important to monitor activity and problems on the network and make adjustments as required. There are additional reasons for this. Because office workstations require interactive use of a network, response time is more critical than with many traditional computer networks. A degradation in the network can result either in total user rejection of the system during a pilot or in important declines in the performance of the organization. As well, as the organization becomes more reliant on the network for its basic functioning, network management grows in importance. In general, the more complex and widespread the network, the greater the importance of network management and the assignment of qualified personnel to this function. Planning for automation in this area is also very important if levels of service are to be maintained.

Technology Policy

The *science* of policy formulation is to determine what approaches to the various facets of planning and implementation will work best. The *art* of policy formulation is to understand when assistance is required and when it is not.

Policy statements were commonly issued by executives in charge of traditional data-processing systems. Typically such statements informed users when computing resources would be available and how systems operations would be handled.

As the enterprise initiates integrated office system planning and implementations, policymakers can provide useful information to end-user departments regarding technical issues in the acquisition and use of integrated systems. In addition to information, it is often appropriate to provide more structured recommendations, guidelines, policies, standards and regulations regarding technology which has corporate-wide implications.

The Issue of Policy

The first thing to realize is that there is no one "best" policy. Policies will be quite different, because of a number of variables:

- **Size of the Organization.** A policy for the central planning body of a large state government will obviously be quite different from that of a small law office with fifteen people.
- **Time.** Policies will vary over time. For example, in the early days of office systems planning, when an organization is unsure about its general direction, it may make more sense to provide end-user departments with information as opposed to rigid standards and policies. As the organization becomes more confident and clearer on the various areas of technical policy, more formal guidelines and standards may be implemented.

- **Structure of the Organization.** Organizations which are highly centralized in their structure may be able to implement more formal policies than organizations which are highly decentralized.
- **Management Style.** Enterprises which encourage autonomous decisionmaking within various end-user departments, for example, may decide that less formal policies are appropriate.
- **Rapidity of Technical Growth.** Policies may make more sense in an organization that is rapidly expanding its technological base than in a company that has slower growth of systems.
- **Existing Relationship between MIS and End-User departments.** In situations where various departments are hostile or antagonistic towards the MIS department, formal standards and regulations may not be possible or desirable.
- **Resources Available.** Formulation of good policy requires considerable senior management resources. If these are not available it may make more sense to concentrate on getting useful information to end-user departments.

Figure 10.1 illustrates the range of options. At one end of the policy continuum, senior management can simply provide information to end-user departments. Moving along the continuum it may be possible to provide informal recommendations. Even farther, formal guidelines or recommendations may be issued. Finally, at the other end of the continuum, it may be possible and desirable for senior management to issue formal policies, standards, and regulations which will be subject to corporate enforcement.

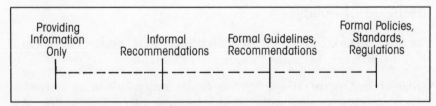

Figure 10.1 The Policy Continuum

The challenge is to determine in what areas and to what degree it is necessary, desirable and helpful to encourage or require things to be the same across the organization. It is also essential to understand the degree to which policies will be accepted by end-user departments. How a department is approached should depend on both the organization's need for things to be the same and the department's openness to technology. As Figure 10.2 illustrates, when both need and acceptance are high, then

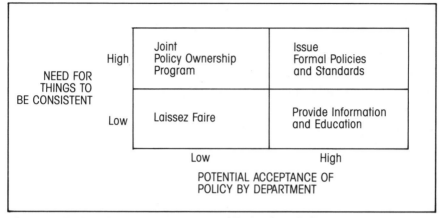

Figure 10.2   Need versus Acceptance of Technology Policy

formal policies and standards are desirable. When both need and acceptance are low, a laissez faire approach is advisable. When need is high and acceptance low, it makes sense to undertake a program whereby senior management works with the management of various departments in formulating mutually acceptable policies. Where need is low but potential acceptance of policies is high, senior management should be providing useful information and educational programs for end-user departments who appear to be seeking guidance.

Another point to note is that there will be multiple policymakers. Policy can be issued from senior management, from the data processing or management information systems department or from various user departments. Other potential sources include the purchasing department, human resources and the physical plant management. The need here is to identify the correct or appropriate source of policy, and to ensure that key potential policymakers are involved in the formulations of any standards or guidelines.

Potential areas where policies may be appropriate include technical standards, security and confidentiality, systems operations and vendor selection. Policies in non-technical areas such as human resource management, the work environment, and implementation of systems may be required as well.

Technology Standards

When it comes to technical standards, organizations can range from what could be called technical anarchy to a technical dictatorship where there is Orwellian uniformity of all technology within the organization.

There are advantages to uniformity. For example, there may be benefits to all employees in the organization using the same technology. There will be standardized training across the organization, supported software, standardized documentation, as well as the benefits derived from standardized tools such as electronic messaging, calendaring, and scheduling. Tradeoffs include the fact that some systems may be inappropriate for some user departments. Standards can result in unnecessary or undesirable restrictions. The organization may move more slowly in its acquisition of technology than is desirable.

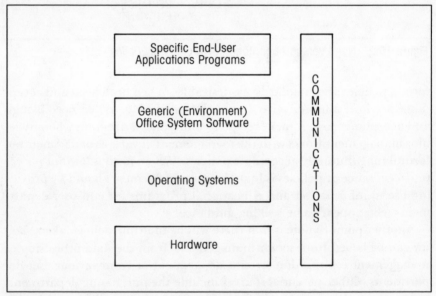

Figure 10.3 Levels of Technical Standardization

Figure 10.3 illustrates a number of possible levels of technology standards. One level is **communications standards**. It makes a lot of sense to adopt an overall corporate network architecture that includes protocols and standards that can best facilitate full, open systems within the organization. This may include the adoption of standard protocols at the lower levels of the Open Systems Interconnection model discussed in Chapter Nine. They can also include the adoption of protocols which are widely used and which may likely become de facto standards in the marketplace.

Some organizations have adopted **hardware** standards. A typical example is to standardize on one or more personal computers for the entire corporation, as was done in a large number of companies who selected the first IBM PC as their standard.

At a higher level, it may be possible or desirable to have a standard

operating system. To continue the example of personal computers, in recent years MS-DOS has become a highly used or "standard" operating system for single-user personal computers, largely due to the IBM PC. At the same time, UNIX, developed in the early 1970s at Bell Laboratories in the U.S., became widely used as an operating system for multi-user microcomputers as well as larger, mini- or mainframe computers.

The next level of standardization would involve **generic office system software**. This provides all users across the corporation with a common user interface, or software environment. This could include the provision of corporate-wide facilities such as text messaging system or a standard facility for accessing corporate databases.

At a higher level still, it may be desirable to provide **specific end-user application programs** which are standard across the corporation. For example, it may be desirable to provide a standard multi-dimensional spreadsheet so that budgets can be pulled together across the enterprise for senior management decisionmaking. It may also be desirable to develop, from a central location, specific end-user application programs such as an accounting package.

There are a number of advantages and disadvantages of technical standards in each of the areas just outlined.

1. Hardware Standards and Policies

Hardware standards can facilitate compatibility at the bottom of the Open Systems Interconnection model. For example, if everyone in the organization is using the same personal computer, communications are facilitated through standardization in areas such as communications ports. Hardware standardization can also facilitate training; for example, everyone will be using the same keyboard. Other benefits include the large discounts provided by many vendors on quantity purchases of hardware.

On the other hand, the product or products of one vendor may not be the most appropriate for all users. There is, for example, no one "best" personal computer for all people in all situations. Hardware standardization does not fully resolve the compatibility issues, as it really addresses the very bottom of the OSI model. However it should be noted that standardization on a given hardware vendor, with a complete proprietary network architecture which covers all levels of the OSI model, has been beneficial in the past where closed, or single-vendor, systems were possible and feasible for many organizations.

Hardware standardization is also difficult to control in large organizations. In many cases where organizations have developed a policy to standardize on one microcomputer, very often the policy has been ignored as various managers purchased whatever micro they pleased within the framework of their own budget. Today, for many companies it is simply too late to standardize on one vendor, given that a multi-vendor environment exists and has deep roots throughout the enterprise.

2. Standard Operating System

Restricting the number of operating systems which reside on hardware throughout the enterprise has a number of benefits. First, compatibility at lower levels of the OSI model is facilitated. Standardizing an operating system can also drastically reduce the time required to develop special application software, by providing a common development environment which is independent of the hardware. This can reduce duplication of the programming effort across the organization as well as provide some standardization in end-user training, because of a common command syntax.

However, operating system technology is still quite immature and selecting a standard operating system is a guessing game. There can also be inefficiencies on some hardware, as some operating systems are better suited than others. Some operating systems are also better for specific end-user applications than others. For example, some lend themselves well to scientific applications where others are more appropriate for business-oriented applications.

Add to these problems the political and organizational difficulties in getting end-user groups to convert their computer facilities to a new operating system and it becomes clear that standardization in this realm is not a simple matter.

3. Generic Office System Software

A good example of standardized office systems software tools would be a common user interface, where all users of the system are presented, when they log on, with a "universal presentation mode". This could be a standard menu outlining all of the various facilities of the system or it could be an icon-based interface where all users are presented with pictorial images of available facilities. Other examples would be prototyping tools, portable programming languages or standardized software tools to enable microcomputers to access corporate databases held on larger computers. Examples of the latter are:

- Report Writers (for reporting locally on data moved downstream from a host).
- Record Handling (with a capability to pick out a desired set of records based on selection criteria).
- Data Analysis (allowing aggregation analysis of data from the host).

- Graphics (proving a common interface for data).
- Data and File Maintenance (to categorize trace, move, delete and update files).

Generic office systems software can facilitate training as standardized documentation and training packages can be distributed across the organization. Generic tools can also enable uniform reporting from corporate databases. Because a quality, friendly and universal user-interface is easier to use and easier to teach, training can be simplified. Standardization on this level can also enable the development of high utility tools for common corporate applications such as electronic messaging.

However software development in this area is, and will be for some time, relatively immature. Generic office systems software may restrict end-users who prefer a different interface. The more standardized the software used by the organization, the greater the support problems, since updating programs or correcting bugs can be a massive undertaking. The political and organizational difficulties inherent in any software standardization also arise in the case of generic office systems software.

4. Specific End-User Applications

Standardized end-user applications can be developed in a central location or acquired off the shelf. Standardization at this level of software can facilitate training dramatically as corporate-wide training packages and programs can be developed and implemented for everyone. Naturally, standardization at this level can assist with full seven-layer OSI compatibility. Another advantage is that well-developed, well-tested software can be delivered to end-users, so avoiding one of the biggest problems of traditional business personal computing — the development of poor quality software by inappropriate people.

However, coming up with an agreement regarding end-user application software may be difficult. For example, when an organization is using ten different spreadsheet programs there will be at least ten different groups who feel strongly that their spreadsheet approach is the most appropriate. Another problem is that the development of standardized applications can be a massive central development effort requiring considerable resources — running the danger of taking office systems back to the time of traditional data processing where one-, two- or three-year development cycles were not uncommon. Support for such a massive effort of standardized software can also require considerable centralized resources. Moreover, standardization at this level can be restrictive to user departments, forcing them into application packages which may not be most appropriate for their particular needs.

In each of these cases, it is important to weigh the potential benefits of standardization with the potential problems and dangers within the specific context of your organization and its strategic direction for office systems. The goal is to identify corporate-wide requirements which are critical to the implementation of a successful technology strategy and implement appropriate standards or guidelines in these areas. At the same time it is generally best to permit and encourage end-user groups to assess their own specific requirements and acquire or develop tools that are unique to their needs.

Security and Confidentiality

Issues regarding the security and confidentiality of systems, data, people and organizations are appropriate topics for corporate policy. These problems have been generated by the proliferation of independent computing devices throughout the office, in particular the microcomputer, and by the trend towards open systems discussed in an earlier chapter.

More and more people are gaining access to central computing resources such as mainframe computers. Increasing numbers of people have potentially sensitive information on their own desktop. In general there is an increased reliance on the part of the organization on its technology. All of these trends pose a number of dangers. In general there is an increased danger of:

- **Unauthorized Access to Restricted Information.** As computers become linked to local area and wide area networks, access to secure databases from inappropriate personnel inside and outside of the organization is increased.
- **Threats to Data Integrity.** The MIS department, once a secured data sanctuary, now faces the difficult problem of ensuring data accuracy within an open systems environment. The microcomputer is a perfect purveyor of inaccurate and damaging data, either accidentally or otherwise. Because most of the problems occur at the level of data entry, the growth of the workstation infrastructure is causing a growing accuracy problem.
- **Danger of Data Loss Due to Turnover.** As databases become spread throughout an organization, particularly those located on individual micros, the possibility of losing a piece of corporate database when an employee leaves is great. This may not be intentional theft, rather data may be stored on an individual micro in a format using access routines that are only known to the departed employee.

- **Danger of Catastrophic Failure.** As the organization becomes more reliant on technology to conduct more aspects of its business, the consequences of system failure are great. In many ways you're betting the future of your company on the reliability of its systems.
- **Danger of Inappropriate System Monitoring.** A good office system can provide, through its system accounting tools, the capability of monitoring virtually every system-related activity of an individual user. This raises important issues regarding individual privacy and confidentiality of information. There are numerous cases where the keystroke activity of employees was monitored as a way of judging individual performance. As will be discussed further in Chapter Twelve, this often resulted in severe implementation problems, and hostility and rejection by potential users.
- **Increased Danger of Data and System Vandalization.** Because the office workstation spreads computer literacy to a greater number of workers, it has dramatically increased the risk of computer crime in the general sense and vandalization specifically. And because systems are connected to wide area networks, the potential for "hackers" to play with or otherwise vandalize data files has become widely known.

Security and confidentiality is an area where corporate policy can be fairly comprehensive and firmly applied in most organizations. Specific areas are:

1. Data Management
Clear procedures will be required for creating, updating, changing and maintaining corporate databases. While the field of data management has been around for some time, the problems of data management created by micros on the one hand and open systems on the other are new and require some innovative and comprehensive approaches. For example, it may make sense to secure all locations where the corporate database resides and to download copies to end-user departments and end-users. At the same time strict control over direct access to these copies of the database must be maintained.

2. Password, File and System Security
Most systems require some kind of password identification to log on. Most also have some kind of optional security on individual files such as a letter, report, spreadsheet file, or text message. Most systems also have some kind of "super-user" security procedures where an authorized system administrator or owner can access all parts of the system. It makes sense to

adopt corporate policies regarding minimal security requirements in all three of these areas.

3. Documentation
All important software, whether purchased or developed on a mainframe or an individual end-user's micro, should be documented. Such documentation must explain what the software does, how data in any data file is organized, and how to use the program.

4. Physical Access and Storage
In the age of the computer center, elaborate security precautions could be taken to prevent unauthorized access to secure facilities. However with a computer on the desktop of all categories of people in the office, the problem becomes more complex. It may, therefore, be a good idea to ensure that storage devices such as disks and tapes containing sensitive data are locked in secure areas at night, terminals are not left logged on when users are away from the office, local area network cable is not run through insecure areas of a building (such as false ceilings, in hallways or ductwork in garages), and similar policies.

5. Backup and Recovery
Corporate policies should specify the frequency and procedures for various levels of back-up of the system; that is, copying of the data which has been created on the system. When one considers that all the information generated by the entire organization may be lost in a significant system failure, it may make sense to have more frequent back-ups than the weekly or daily back-up used for data-processing systems. As well, procedures for disaster recovery and policies regarding duplication and off-site storage of critical data should be formulated.

6. System Monitoring
In most instances, monitoring an individual employee's activities on the system is counterproductive. Setting aside ethical considerations, the information gained is generally far outweighed by the damage done in employee morale, labor relations and user acceptance. It therefore makes sense to have corporate policies, which are widely publicized, regarding exactly what monitoring will be conducted and to what purposes such monitoring or accounting data will be applied. For example, system accounting data from employees who are responding to customer inquiries and problems may be useful in helping to understand general trends between branches or regions, across products or service types and so on.

But a good corporate policy would assure these employees that such accounting data would not be used for individual performance evaluation.

Vendor Selection

The August 1983 issue of *Business Week* had a cover story entitled "Computer Shock, A Wide Proliferation Hits the Office — Confusing Buyers, Sellers and Managers". The article pointed out that managers, fed up with corporate computer centers requiring months to do a job, were taking matters into their own hands by buying their own machines. However, after being inundated by some two hundred makers of personal computers, most managers were being overwhelmed by "option shock".

There's no reason to believe the situation is going to improve, considering that the vendors of computers, office and telecommunications equipment are all on a migration path towards the target market of integrated office systems. The potential market to directly support all categories of people who work in the office makes the old data processing, office products and even telecommunications market look miniscule.

In the scramble for markets, there is a continual shakedown in which only the fittest survive. This has made the process of vendor selection more treacherous and at the same time has led many organizations to be more conservative, selecting only mainstream vendors. This has often been quite frustrating as very often the mainstream vendors do not provide the most appropriate products for both immediate and projected needs.

For several reasons, the issue of vendor selection should become, in part, an issue of corporate policy. First, the selection of technology by end-user departments may have important ramifications for the technical infrastructure of the organization as a whole. Second, as the importance of technology increases, the issue of selecting the most appropriate vendor or mix of vendors becomes a strategic issue which is critical to the success of the enterprise. Third, end-user department personnel are often not experienced enough or equipped to make the most appropriate selections and can fall prey to the sales pitches of vendors with weak products and product strategies. Fourth, the criteria which must be applied to the vendor selection process are being improved constantly and are beginning to include considerations which are best assessed at an overall corporate level.

Having said this, it should be pointed out that there is a tension between the need for overall corporate policy in this area and the need to provide end-user departments with adequate freedom to assess their requirements and select vendors which correspond to their particular situation.

Policies for Analysis and Evaluation

During the earlier days of data processing, methods for assessing user requirements, cost justifying, and evaluating systems focused on identifying opportunities for cost displacement and cost avoidance. These methods were designed and implemented by central Systems Analysis, Work Simplification or Methods personnel, or possibly outside consultants. The end-user and end-user management tended to be the object or recipient of these methods.

Because the methods focused on identifying opportunities to more efficiently process structured information, a structured design of the new system or procedure was formulated and then a new system constructed, sometimes after many months had passed by. Often the new system did not correspond to the requirements of the end-users as time had intervened to change the situation, or as the approach taken was highly limited. The notion of "technology driven" systems became a popular way of describing systems that were designed, somewhat in a vacuum, without adequate consideration of what the end-users required and would accept.

Somewhat in response to this problem, many end-users and user departments purchased microcomputers for themselves in an attempt to get systems which more closely corresponded to their requirements. However, often these computers were again purchased in the absence of real information regarding the requirements of the user.

The initiation of integrated office systems pilots introduces the need for new and sound methods for assessing user requirements and designing office systems. To avoid the problems of the past, it makes sense for senior management to provide assistance to departments in determining their office system needs. This assistance can range anywhere from providing *information* about good approaches and methods to establishing *policies and standards* which must be followed by all departments.

Indeed some form of information or policy can be useful in regard to the very *process* of assessing department requirements and evaluating the impact of department pilots, and also concerning the *methods* for such assessment.

The process of assessing requirements and evaluation is changing compared to traditional data-processing systems analysis or word-processing analysis. There is a shift towards more participative methods of designing systems, which involve the potential users fully in the process of change.

This means helping the users acquire a better understanding of their organization and their work, along with a common language as a way of winning a sense of user "ownership" of the system design.

Because the new systems are evolutionary — growing from small pilots or other implementations into fuller operational systems — methods must enable evolutionary growth. In particular, methods are needed for evaluating the impact of the system and enabling cost-benefit-analyses for its extension.

As a result, it may be necessary to provide information or adopt corporate policies regarding the process of assessing requirements and evaluating systems. In particular guidelines regarding how users and their organizations, such as unions, should be involved can assist departments in avoiding the pitfalls of a design process which excludes the main stakeholders.

Methodology for Analysis, Cost-Benefit and Evaluation

It is not possible to simply ask users what they need. True, users may have valuable insights into their own problems. However, they are usually not able to identify the system solutions to these and other problems they face, let alone specify in detail, cost-justify and plan an implementation strategy for these solutions. Moreover, subjective measures are simply not adequate to evaluate user requirements. A classic example is time estimation. Secretaries, for example, often estimate that they spend a majority of their day typing, when behavioral measures show the proportion at less than 20 percent.

As a result, it makes good sense to be as scientific as possible in collecting valid and reliable data. No one in their right mind will tell you that this is easy. Clearly, office work, processes and activities are complex, often unstructured and hard to measure. But given that the alternative is to muddle through and design office systems based on impressionistic, unverifiable, and likely, highly controversial information, most advanced organizations have concluded that investing in good methods of analysis is worthwhile.

There are a number of focus shifts for the *methods* used to analyze office systems themselves.

- Methods now focus on assessing opportunities to improve unstructured or semi-structured work, rather than the structured processes addressed by traditional data processing or word processing.
- Office systems are broader in scope than traditional systems, therefore

methods must be more comprehensive, focusing on the social and environmental as well as the technical aspects of the system.

- The thrust of the feasibility analysis has shifted from measuring opportunities for cost-displacement to measuring opportunities to improve the overall performance of the organization. As a result methods must be more sophisticated and complex.
- The importance of *impact assessment* tends to be greater, as the feasibility for major capital expenditures will, in most cases be based on an evaluation of the effects of smaller office systems and pilots.

A good methodology has a number of components.

1. Conceptual Framework
As outlined earlier in Chapter Five, it is important to have a clear conceptual or theoretical approach from which to approach the assessment of user requirements and the evaluation of systems. Rather than taking a "shotgun" approach to assessing opportunities, it is better to know on which types of opportunities you want to focus.

2. Sampling
Selection of the sample for a study seems like a trivial business. It is not. The criteria to be used are not those typically applied to field experiments, for example. Respondents for a requirements analysis will become users. The process of winning respondent cooperation is also a process of winning user acceptance of the system. As a result selection of the sample for a study can be critical to the success of the system. Guidelines regarding involvement of persons from all levels of the organization, from key stakeholder groups, etc., may prove useful.

3. Measurement Instruments
There are a variety of standard *measurement instruments* which can be used and others should be developed. Most categories of instrumentation can be used. These include questionnaires, diaries, logs, key product tracking, information flow modeling, critical incident techniques, secondary source data, communications network analysis, interviews, and observation.

Standard instruments can be supplied across the enterprise and customized, if so desired, by individual departments or user groups. Instruments must be designed in a concrete context, with reference to the system objectives. For example, a good questionnaire which measures employee attitudes and the climate for technological change could be provided to all departments. Maximum use should be made of data collection tools already in place, such as department performance evaluation systems. To avoid the danger of invalid data, or worse, undermining potential user cooperation and support for the system itself, care must be taken not to burden the respondents with obtrusive and time-consuming instruments.

4. Data Analysis

Data analysis will present a formidable challenge. Much of the data analysis will be descriptive, rather than statistical in nature. General statistical analysis programs are available. It may also make sense to develop special programs centrally and make them, or the expertise to analyze data, available to various departments. A good example are Network Analysis programs which have been applied to office systems requirements analysis. These programs help explain the human communications process in an organization and can be invaluable in the selection of pilot groups, individual users and communications tools.

5. Documentation of the Process

Documentation of the analysis and evaluation process serves two purposes: a) it enables an evaluation of the process itself; and b) it protects the project from disruptions due to possible turnover in the project team.

6. User Role in Defining Productivity Measures

The users themselves should take an important role in defining office products, critical success factors and performance measures. The central goal of any implementation is to make an improvement. The users and user management are best equipped to define what constitutes an "improvement" in the context of their organization. There are few, if any, universal productivity measures which are applicable to all organizations, at all times. Office productivity is an abstraction that must be defined concretely, within a given context.

In some cases, users have taken responsibility for quantifying the *value* of defined improvements as well. This can have very positive results as it facilitates the cost-benefit analysis, especially when evaluating the less tangible, but vitally important opportunities created by the new systems.

Measuring the Reinvestment of Time Savings

As has been explained, office systems can have a very positive impact on time use. A good system design will include a reinvestment strategy for saved time. This is a plan regarding how all categories of office personnel in the department can undertake new activities that were not possible before.

A corporate-wide reinvestment strategy will have been developed as part of the Strategic Direction. However, it may be useful to provide information and guidelines for user departments regarding reinvestment *within those departments*. Doing so will help the organization as a whole capture the benefits of time savings and do so in a fashion which is consistent with the overall corporate reinvestment objectives.

STRATEGIES FOR PEOPLE AND CHANGE

4

Implications for Human Resource Management

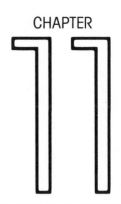

Of the three architectures — technology, social and environmental — which must be designed for the new work system, the social is the one most often ignored in the planning stages. We take for granted that the social fabric of the enterprise will adapt to whatever changes occur; that people will come to fit into their new situation.

Only after the pilot has failed do we realize the difficult truth: unless the technological and environmental choices made take into account the needs of the people, the new integrated systems won't work. (Figure 11.1 illustrates their interrelationship.) These human imperatives must be respected, especially when it comes to job design, organizational restructuring and training. This argument is made, not from a perspective of

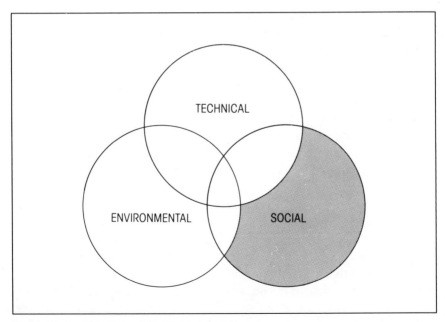

Figure 11.1 The Role of the Social Architecture

ethics or morality, but from a hard-nosed, pragmatic business point of view. Failure to resolve the human resource implications of integrated office systems has time and again proven to be a terrible and costly *business* mistake.

Many traditional work systems that involved computers were designed according to Frederick Taylor's 1885 Theory of Scientific Management. Taylor held that a good work system was one where each individual did one structured task, tightly supervised, with little autonomy and with intrinsic motivators like salary or fear of punishment. Many word-processing centers, keypunch departments and computer programming shops were designed according to the Taylorist model. This approach has been found lacking when applied to integrated office systems. In fact, it just doesn't work, especially when compared to new approaches to designing high performance work systems which involve extensive use of sophisticated technology.

New Channels, New Relationships

Most of the work we do in offices is done along with other people: bosses, peers, subordinates. Just how closely we work with others depends on the type of work, our own preferences, and the various carrots offered by the organization's formal and informal reward system.

Whatever the case, the introduction of the new systems can, and probably will, change the social relationships in an office. For our key link with our co-workers is communications — and communication via computers is changing the way people interact. For example, these new systems present opportunities to increase the frequency and effectiveness of communications, allowing different people to talk to each other, share resources, information and ideas.

Such corporate networks can go far beyond the mere transfer of data to the actual creation and exchange of knowledge, with incredible benefits for the organization. Access to both information and the people in the organization is enhanced and so is the probability of making sound decisions, which can have a positive economic and social impact on the organization.

The more open the network, the greater the number of possible combinations of people and ideas, creating a climate for unlimited innovation and creativity. Yet chances of chaos taking over are minimized by the fact that each person in the network remains in control of their own particular contribution. This benefits both the organization and the individual. When people feel they have control over their work, they feel greater responsibility for its quality. And as part of a well-designed work system they can be considerably more productive.

At the other extreme, the individual may have little or no control over the information communicated by the new work systems. Witness the experience of telephone operators who are very closely monitored as a result of the introduction of automated equipment. The system keeps track of the average time it takes an operator to handle a call, and management has set strict standards for performance.

Such close monitoring can be devastating to the health of employees, inducing stress, health problems and feelings of powerlessness and even complete apathy. As a result, organizational productivity can plummet, even though it may appear that the standards are being met. Say an operator is supposed to take no longer than twenty-six seconds to handle your call. If she cuts you off before that amount of time has elapsed, she's made her deadline — at your expense.

The problem is not the fact that such information can be collected and communicated. Take another example in a similar area, that of word-processing operators and their equipment. While it is possible to keep track of every keystroke done on the operator's work system, if this information is automatically fed to supervisors, then the word-processing operator is in the same position as the telephone operator.

But it doesn't have to be this way. Imagine a quite different scenario. The supervisor leaves a message for the word-processing operator, explaining that the department is looking into the pros and cons of redesigning jobs so that no one will be expected to spend an entire workday entering text into the system. For this purpose, it would be helpful to measure the number of keystrokes entered on an average day by one operator working full time and compare this rate to that of several operators working for two-hour periods. The operator willingly agrees to participate, in fact even suggesting that the survey be conducted next week instead, since a lot of the fastest operators are out sick this week.

Too often in the past we have used very narrow criteria in the design of work technology, such as ease of learning, operator fatigue and safety. A good argument can be made for broadening these criteria to include factors such as individual autonomy, social connectedness, meaningful work and effective participation, that is, a voice in decisionmaking.

Standards can be set so designers of the new work systems can judge what human effects are to be considered good, bad or neutral, and which are to be considered of particular importance. Then the impact of any proposed design on the people in the organization must be assessed. What changes will it require in terms of job design, organizational procedures and structure, or training programs? Will it increase the degree of specialization necessary, require new skills, or change the reporting relationships and flow of information within the organization? In turn, these changes will affect the motivation and personal development of the people in the enterprise and lead to either social conflict or to organizational harmony.

Your predictions may be off in some cases, but at least you'll have a record of your expectations to compare with the actual results. Also, you'll have a valuable picture of the enterprise prior to the introduction of any change. Without this it is much more difficult to tell what problems were actually caused by the new systems. As Mary Baetz points out in her book *The Human Imperative: Planning for People in the Integrated Office*, it is important to create and communicate organizational human resource policies *before* problems present themselves. For one thing is sure, during the implementation of the new technologies any weaknesses in the existing systems (such as reward or performance) will stick out like a sore thumb and *the problem will be attributed to the new technology*.

Changing Power Relationships

New communications channels can also change the power relationships in the organization. A new channel can give power to an individual or a group by limiting the access of others to information or by selectively distorting the information transmitted. Whereas access to information used to be limited, these new systems provide, at least potentially, equal access for all persons. At the same time, the significance of this change is being recognized, and in some organizations, the battle lines are being drawn.

For example, in one organization, a large union, the president was initially concerned that any office system implementation be controlled by his office rather than the administration division. The latter group had the officially delegated responsibility for communications, word and data processing. The concern was clearly one of ensuring that information was given only to those who had a need to know, and then perhaps only in a limited fashion.

Organizational power in the 1980s may reside with those persons who make decisions about how integrated office systems will interact with the structure, goals, communication patterns and the existing tools within a particular organization.

Information is a tool of power, an element in obtaining and retaining power. Timely information is invaluable in setting goals to retain power. The integrated office system is a revolutionary change in both the source of power and in the tools for actualizing power in organizations. Hence, the decisions related to the planning, development, installation and management of the new work systems will be a focal point for the power struggle in organizations for the foreseeable future.

Organization Structures Are Changing

Many organizations today are structured with a wide base of workers controlled by an increasingly smaller number of managers. As a result of the new systems, a new, flatter structure seems to be evolving, a matrix form. In this case a person may report to a number of people, depending on the needs of the organization at any specific time. One's position in relation to others is no longer as important, and is in fact overridden by the ability to communicate information directly to people regardless of their position. As discussed in the previous section, real power in the organization is largely determined by access to information.

In truth, many organizations have always ignored the formal organizational chart that was supposed to govern them, operating according to an informal, unwritten order that was soon transmitted to all newcomers. The point is that all organizations are structured in some way and that this structure will both affect and be affected by the new technologies.

Let's have a look at how an enterprise can reorganize itself for the introduction of integrated office systems. In the case of a financial management organization, the success of the firm depended on maximizing the professional time and effectiveness of the funds managers. The administration department was therefore responsible for providing accurate and up-to-date information for decisionmaking and an extensive and effective communications system.

To manage the rapid growth of this organization and meet the day-to-day decisionmaking requirements, an organization superstructure was created by asking employees to perform their own line job and sit on one of four policy committees: employee relations, compensation benefits, training and systems operations. In addition, three other groups were formed including funds managers, decisionmakers, and employees at large. Each of these groups was assigned a chairperson. The heads of all seven groups came together through an advisory council and all decisions made in the firm went through this council.

Typical line decisions were market-timing trading decisions, internal accounting and computer vendor selection. Policy committees made decisions in their areas of specialization: training, compensation and benefits, hiring and promotion, organizational design, structure and job content.

Within the organization there was also an information coordinator who reported to the administrator and therefore had no direct role in the superstructure. In theory such a person should not be biased by the issues dealt with by the policy committees and representative groups. The coordinator's main job was to keep employees informed of day-to-day activities, track decisionmaking processes and communications and generally encourage employees to take a role in issues requiring their decision. Indeed, this type of organization has resulted in greater knowledge of company activities on the part of all employees and broader participation in decisionmaking.

The new organizational structure and process was designed to work optimally with new technology. The change in technology and structure go hand in hand. One wouldn't work well without the other.

Well-designed data-processing systems first rationalized the manual process and then automated it. Well-designed office systems integrate support technologies *as part of* the redesign of the work system. The difference is subtle but critical.

This change in emphasis and approach can be factored into a plan. At the corporate level new organizational structures may be anticipated as part of the planning process. For example, it may be foreseen that the system will obviate the need for regional offices or a given function within the enterprise. New structures, to take advantage of new business opportunities generated by the plan, may be predicted.

In a smaller business, the responsibility for implementing integrated office systems would most likely be assumed by the president, vice president or perhaps the office manager of the organization.

Organizational conflicts and jurisdictional battles are less likely to be a problem. The issue will most probably be what systems the small business can plug into and how this might best be accomplished. Then the question is what roles which persons should play in implementing these new integrated office systems.

In the case of professionals, the issue may be how to become part of a larger network, and have access to information and services. This would apply particularly to physicians, nurses and other medical support personnel in clinics. For example, via a network doctors may have access from their clinic to hospital facilities where they can obtain general and medical information or even up-to-date patient information.

Whatever the size of the business, solving the organizational issues requires a clear vision of organizational goals and objectives. If the people within the organization are not open to new ideas that may benefit the enterprise as a whole, a view from the outside world, such as that of a consultant, may help.

The Role of Unions

Because of the traditional adversarial relationship which exists between unions and management, many organizations are reluctant to involve their unions in the early stages of technological change. While some firms allow unions to participate in the implementation of the new systems, they draw the line at letting organized labor have a voice in the design of the work system itself. The feeling is that management alone is responsible for making sure the company remains competitive.

Of course unions also have an interest in ensuring the long-term viability and economic stability of their companies. They also have a real contribution to make to the design process, especially when it comes to redesigning jobs and providing retraining for people whose jobs have changed. Indeed without this support at the beginning, the success of the implementation is seriously jeopardized.

In the case of a large telephone company, management sought the cooperation of its major operator union in the conversion of operator positions to an automated system, requesting union participation in the design of the new workstations. However, management solicited less assistance in the job design itself and failed to redesign the supervisory positions to manage the new work environment. It was not until after an operator strike, one of the few in the history of the company, that management saw the need to change their current style. Had the union been consulted on the issue of job redesign, job satisfaction might well have been considerably increased. Paradoxically, few operators would now choose to return to the former working environment if given the option.

So a case must be made for the involvement of unions, as labor relations issues are key to the introduction of the new systems. While this is not commonly accepted in North America, union participation in office systems design is the norm in some European countries, in particular, Scandinavia.

What if the unions argue strongly against the introduction of new technology for their employers, either because of fear of job loss or the associated risks to health and safety? Despite a reluctant labor force and continued industrial strife, along with organizational resistance to change, there is an opportunity for the employer to achieve harmony and produce a socially acceptable program. The degree of resistance within the organization should be determined and reflected in a well-thought-out education program.

Remember also that growing memberships, demand for services and information are forcing unions to look to the new office systems for their own communications and information requirements. Employers are implementing systems for use in bargaining — giving negotiators immediate access to corporate data-banks and decision-support systems. And, because of rising unemployment, declining union membership in some sectors and effective anti-union campaigns by business and government, unions are combining to acquire the required strength in bargaining for contracts.

Although many of the unions within unions are hostile to the introduction of such systems because of past disastrous experience, they also recognize that without these new systems they may not survive, let alone thrive.

Strategies for People

New technology does not automatically result in higher productivity. The critical component is the way in which it is managed. This means assessing any new procedure in light of the whole job, and in turn assessing the job in terms of the employees' expectations regarding job satisfaction and career mobility.

A positive orientation to managing automation should be a matter of organizational policy rather than a random event. The critical point is to manage the context of the job. Employees should feel they are working in a humane and trusting environment and that they are being treated fairly. Employees should also participate in the design of the work procedures, decisions about work standards, as well as have a voice in decisions affecting changes to the more general physical and social environment.

In an article entitled "Race Against Time", Judith Gregory has argued forcefully that office automation will have a profound impact upon the white collar working force. She is concerned primarily with lower level administrative positions and sees the impact as threefold: taking a dull job and making it even more boring, taking a dull job and making it easier to accomplish, or eliminating the job altogether.[1]

Others take a more positive view and believe the new technology will bring about job enrichment through the elimination of tedious work, thereby freeing up time for more interesting tasks. Which view is right depends very much on how the technology evolves and on how adequately job design and redesign is handled when introducing the new work systems.

The problem is that is all too easy to confuse the different dimensions of the issue. However, before we can manage the introduction of the new technologies, we must sort out exactly what can be controlled and what can't.

First, there are the consequences of automation arising from factors inherent in the technology itself. For example, consider how the computer itself changes the way a person and task are related.

The person now must work through an office system rather than directly on the specific task at hand. In consequence, that person is working with symbols of the work to be done, not the actual task itself. So the computer stands between the person and the real work to be done, as a mediator.

Computer-mediated work also introduces new performance requirements on the job: in some cases, such as skilled jobs, the ability to analyze data becomes more important than practical know-how. What this means is that managing computer-mediated work involves rethinking the nature of work, its purpose and optimum work behavior. For example, traditional supervisory concerns may no longer be important as the focus becomes one of responding to information. New roles will emerge, such as ensuring employees have access to the data they need.

The point is that jobs *will* have to be redesigned, people will have to be retrained because of the new technologies. *How* this will be accomplished is in no way determined by the technology itself.

Next, as part of a plan, it is up to the firm to decide what statement the computer-based system will make about management assumptions and values regarding employee motivation and commitment.[2] Systems which monitor employee performance on a minute-to-minute basis reflect a very low opinion of how employess think and what is required to obtain high productivity. Unless managers become much more aware of the values they build into the system and the consequences of their designs, they themselves will eventually be confronted with new methods of monitoring as their work becomes mediated by computers.

A critical issue, given the economic climate in which managers must operate, is job security. Because the price of technology is falling at a time when increased productivity is essential, it cannot be denied that the new office systems will create changes, particularly at the administrative level. The number of clerks who could be displaced from their current jobs may be considerable, and careful consideration must be given to how these people may be retrained for a different or higher level of work. At other levels the nature of work is also beginning to change. With the advent of Expert Systems — systems using artificial intelligence techniques to improve or replace the work of various kinds of experts — we can anticipate even more profound impacts.

Again, during the implementation of new work systems, all members of the enterprise will be closely watching to see how this issue is managed. Because everyone realizes office automation may mean the elimination of some jobs, many companies are making a commitment to job security, and are assuring employees that retraining programs are available so relocation in another part of the organization is possible. Some firms are going one step further and planning career paths for personnel within their own area of expertise.

Of course, not all companies will be able to make these promises as part of an integrated office sytems plan. Some jobs will disappear or be altered drastically, reduced to a series of simple tasks. Many fears of the implementation of the new technologies are very real — just witness the case of the telephone operator or processor of claims forms. Yet the introduction of the new technologies does not have to be this way; there are choices to be made. Figure 11.2 illustrates the potential dangers — and the potential payoffs of integrated office systems.

Which of the potential "dangers" or the "payoffs" occur depends on the plan and how it is implemented. Policies can be implemented in each of these areas to ensure that the dangers are avoided and that the organization achieves the maximum productivity improvements.

DANGERS	POTENTIAL BENEFITS
1. Job loss	1. Job change/new career paths
2. Deskilling — task work	2. Multi-function work
3. Increased monitoring and control	3. Privacy, autonomy and participation
4. Dangers to health and safety	4. Improved work environment
5. Reinforced sex discrimination	5. New opportunities for women
6. Reduced overall quality of work life	6. Improved quality of work life
7. Decreased personal productivity	7. Improved personal effectiveness

Figure 11.2 Dangers and Potential of Integrated Office Systems

Challenges to the Human Resources Manager

Any organization that has a Human Resources group, should involve it in the development of integrated office systems. For unless the Human Resources manager is directly involved in the planning process, she or he will be unable to rise to the planning challenge.

Someone in the organization will have to take responsibility for championing human and organizational aspects of the new systems, and the more experience such a person has in this area, the better. New systems will require new training programs, the development of new job descriptions, new pay scales, as well as assistance for individual employees in overcoming personal resistance and making the transition to the new systems.

Although there are many common issues, it may be necessary, especially during initial implementations, to pay special attention to the needs of administrative and non-management employees, especially women. This is true particularly when the new technologies may require considerable job retraining or the acquisition of new job skills. Human resources managers may also have to assist in developing new work groups and in reorganizing reporting relationships, expecially at the lower levels of the organization.

To date, the focus has been on routine types of office tasks, such as forms processing and order handling. Yet it is the non-routine tasks such as decisionmaking and negotiating that present the greatest opportunity for advanced computing and communications systems. So the human resources manager will at times be breaking new ground, attempting to design jobs and systems of interrelated activity which suit the complexity of their environment.

This is not to say that the final solutions need be complicated. Simple approaches such as the development of coalitions may be the answer to very complex planning dilemmas. In this case, the challenge to the human resource manager is to see that the policies which reward and encourage team participation are also developed. For without appropriate performance appraisal and reward systems each employee will continue to work in directions counter to the collective goal.

Many organizations today in North America appear to be undergoing a fundamental shift in values which is being expressed in the creation of jobs to fit the people, encouragement of worker participation, and development of shared goals. Employees are being encouraged to accept change generally, undertake more risks, and develop an entrepreneurial attitude. Finally, there is the recognition that long-range efficiency and effectiveness depends on today's concern for a harmonious work environment, employee health and excellent customer relations. The human resources manager can help the company achieve these goals, even in a time of continuing technological change.

Job Design

Designing jobs for the office of the future is no easy task, yet it is the key to a successful implementation. For the overall objectives of the business unit to be met, it is necessary to determine the tasks which must be performed and to combine these into satisfying jobs.

You must also be careful not to confuse the performance of a number of office tasks with the underlying office function, automating the former and expecting an improvement in the latter. For example, you may provide tools such as automated forms processing for accounts payable and receivable. This does not necessarily mean you can expect an improvement in the overall function of accounting.

Too much of the effort to increase productivity has focused on work which is single rather than multiple task: the number of calls handled by an operator or forms processed by an insurance clerk. In truth, only jobs with multiple tasks *can* benefit from the process of office automation.

For example, integrated office systems will ultimately eliminate the more routine, clerical types of tasks performed by the administrative staff and create more interesting ones. For professionals and managers, it means removing time consuming and repetitive tasks such as budget preparation, which increases the time and opportunity to run through more scenarios before making an operational decision. For employees whose entire job revolves around the single routine task which is eliminated, such as typesetting, so is their job.

Even professionals or highly skilled technicians can be affected. Some organizations may use the system to program decisionmaking rather than augmenting it, or use it to draw technical diagrams. In either case, jobs will disappear.

Even when jobs are not lost, individual productivity (i.e., number of calls handled) may not necessarily translate into an overall improvement in corporate productivity (how many customers were cut off?). In order to bring this about, proper job redesign must be implemented to ensure that the newly automated work tasks are not repetitive and boring for the user. The interrelationships which exist from one job to another must also be examined to ensure proper coordination of work activity. The redesign must begin *before* the new system is implemented and be carried on even after implementation, in response to an ongoing evaluation.

Integrated office systems can often result in considerable reductions in the time required to complete a particular task. For example, the time to create and revise a report can be reduced by giving users direct access to text preparation facilities. Or the amount of time required to communicate a piece of information can be reduced, and the accuracy of delivery improved, through the use of a messaging facility which does not require the other person to be there to receive the message. The time made available (a "soft" dollar benefit) can be reinvested in other tasks either delegated from above or initiated by the person. The proper reinvestment of time is critical if in fact these "soft dollar" savings are to be realized.

In one Canadian organization whose main product is research reports sold to the public, a careful examination of the process of creating these reports indicated that the total timeframe extended over two years. By carving out one part of this process, which took 122 days, and reexamining it in light of a new integrated office system, it was possible to reduce the time down to eighteen working days. The changes to jobs were dramatic. Secretarial positions evolved into those of administrative assistants, with a greater report production. The tasks of the professional writers, in this case primarily engineers, were enhanced by giving them direct access to a text processing system where they could enter and edit text. Numerous feedback loops were eliminated. *The net result was that the organization was able to undertake additional activities with the same number of employees.*

In another case, that of a large international commercial financial institution, it was possible to change the amount of time loans officers were actually doing productive work from 9% of their day to 50% by reorganizing the flow of administrative paperwork and providing automated tools to handle much of the paperwork in a more efficient and effective manner.

Such examples illustrate the real potential of job design, not narrowly focused lower level clerical and administrative office jobs. Boredom, repetition, uninteresting job content and confusing VDT jobs have all been proven to create feelings of worker dissatisfaction. Jobs reoriented to the new technology too often require workers to stay at their workspace for long periods and the pacing is determined by the machine. Performance monitoring is controlled more by the machine than the supervisor, and this can lead to considerable emotional stress. The situation is further compounded by social isolation, a lack of identification with the end product, and a loss of self-esteem. But it doesn't have to be this way. The new systems can be designed to enrich both jobs and careers.

While job satisfaction and similar feelings can only be determined in relation to a particular job and person, we do have some idea of the attributes which are necessary to provide a highly motivating work situation. First, the job content itself must be motivation for the worker. That is, it should require a variety of skills to produce a product (or service) that is complete and identifiable, that is relevant to both the worker and the organization.

The introduction of the new systems should not be used as an opportunity to deskill jobs or reduce financial remuneration to employees through reclassification. In most cases, we anticipate that jobs can be enhanced with a variety of new tasks and that this may even warrant appropriate upgrading of salaries.

Another important dimension in job redesign is the degree of autonomy allowed. Keep in mind that the more responsibility a person is given in deciding how to do his or her work, the better, in terms of motivation. A similar effect is produced by building participative decisionmaking groups.

To put it simply, people who are trusted within the framework of a well-designed work system usually work harder to live up to that expectation. Any company that chooses the other route, monitoring every move, will probably find that the employees perform as expected, repaying the obvious distrust with sabotage, either blatant or subtle.

Finally, you cannot expect employees who are fearful for their jobs to work to maximum potential. In trying to secure their own positions, they may in fact be working contrary to the best interest of the organization. As discussed earlier, organizational policies regarding job security must be established. Where it is impossible to guarantee the continuity of any one job, no matter how well designed, an organizational commitment to retraining employees for other positions should be considered.

Businesses that ignore the human and organizational requirements of office automation often fail to budget for the costs of redesign and retraining. Later, they are shocked to discover that these costs can equal those of the systems themselves. The bottom line is that any firm which cannot afford these costs cannot really afford the new technologies.

Retraining and Career Paths

While it is all well and good to decide to motivate employees with new tasks and responsibilities, that is only the first step. New training programs must be provided as well for many people affected by the implementation of an integrated office system.

Sometimes office automation may require fewer people to do a job, so the question is who should be retrained? Management can take a very positive approach here and use training to bridge the gap between job redesign and new career paths. Imperial Oil, for example, has retrained employees for new careers within the same organizational division, or even in other parts of the organization entirely.

The issue of long-term careers for women in the workforce deserves some additional attention. Women in North America make up approximately 40% of the workforce. Two-thirds of these women are in the office sector, in the clerical and secretarial jobs which are targets of the new technologies. There is little evidence to show that streaming of women into traditional jobs is changing due to the technology, indeed, it is more likely to be the opposite.

In traditional data processing women have been channeled into lower level jobs. Women account for 95% of data entry clerks, 75% of machine operators and 62% of peripheral equipment operators.

Traditional systems were designed to streamline work by creating task jobs such as keypunch or word processing. As we move into this new technological era of integrated office systems and provide workers with multifunctional tools which can assist in their information handling and communications activities, there are considerable opportunities to change these roles for women.

One job group which has seen a positive impact on career paths has been women in administrative support functions. Women who have gained knowledge in the word-processing centers are a very real source of expertise for the overall office automation effort.

In one case, a woman who was a secretary in a research and development organization was able to quickly learn how to use a new office system when it was introduced. She quickly became a reference source for others in the organization. Subsequently, she was promoted to be in charge of all system training for the organization, and ultimately left to become the manager of office automation for a small oil company. Such paths are becoming increasingly common.

In another case, a secretary who saw the potential for office systems put herself on a self-motivated course to learn all she could about the new systems. She was eventually perceived as an "innovator" within the organization, and was first put in charge of the company word-processing center and later promoted into the office automation group as a consultant and system implementor.

Working in traditional word-processing environments has often also been a springboard to other departments, for example:

- Methods and Procedures analyst
- Telecommunications specialist
- Administrative Support manager
- Personnel and Training manager
- Information Center specialist

Higher up the organizational ladder, office automation managers are beginning to recognize the importance of technical career paths. Not only does the individual benefit from additional training, but so does the organization. New skills can mean improved productivity and the ability to undertake new services.

At the same time, you should recognize that the lack of new training and a solid career ladder may mean the loss of personnel to another organization, often at a very high cost to the firm.

Alternative Work Patterns

The impacts of office automation affect not just what people do, but also how, when and where they do it. With new methods of communications and ways of accessing information, the new technologies are providing employees with opportunities to work from home and other locations external to the office itself.

According to a 1982 report by the Diebold Group, there are several reasons for the increased interest in remote work options: workspace facilities and costs are often in short supply, particularly in large urban centers; it is becoming more difficult to attract and retain qualified personnel; travel energy and commuting costs are rising; and advances in computer/communications technology have increased the potential for telecommuting.

Some have argued that working from remote locations is a perfectly logical step in the way work is defined and organized. In the future, they say, work may be characterized by contracts (paid by fees rather than wages), organizational dispersion (due to the economy of moving information out rather than bringing resources to a central point), greater personal control of work, and labor substituting for energy. Alvin Toffler predicts that the businesses that will prosper will learn how to customize their products and services at the lowest cost with the latest technology. He is an advocate of the "electronic cottage", which can indeed sound quite idyllic.

Others, such as Studs Terkel, point out that one of the main joys of work is "schmoozing" — or that sense of companionship and togetherness workers share as they chat about their lives, complain about common problems, or talk about their jobs. This benefit may not survive if the office moves to the home. Survival will depend upon building institutions and channels that will maintain human contact when the office is moved home. At the office we are forced to think about others rather than ourselves. This shift provides a key link with society as we are able to develop a sense of team spirit and participation in something larger than the individual. At the office, a spirit can develop which says "we are all in this together" and this in turn inspires the dedication and discipline to accomplish the work at hand.

It must also be recognized that the physical separation of officeworkers presents a "transaction barrier". Studies conducted at IBM offices indicated that when workers are physically separated, communications are reduced considerably. For example, moving people a floor apart can cut contact by 90%. In essence, "out of sight, out of mind." It is difficult to know if the new communications tools of an electronic office will alter such trends significantly. Evidence from the widespread use of electronic mail and computer conferencing systems suggests so.

Richard Harkness, in a report published by the Stanford Research Institute, suggests that extensive use of teleconferencing may undermine critical aspects of business relationships. We could become a world of specialists at a superficial level, with the deeper relationships normally established in business no longer occurring. Remote management could change the superior-subordinate relationship, exacerbating problems which already exist in current offices. Finally, the report suggests that company loyalty may decline as a result of geographical remoteness. At the same time, identification with the neighbors and professional peers one does see personally may increase.

Others, like John Naisbitt, agree that techniques like teleconferencing are unlikely to be popular because, as human beings, we want to be in the company of others, and indeed we want to go to the office.

An organization's future direction will be an important factor in determining the success of telecommuting. For while the technology can be used to allow greater participation in decisionmaking, it can also be used to exploit the centralization of organizations. The need to be located near the center of power for career reasons may be a major roadblock to telenetworks.

Work-at-home programs may create changes in family structure (on the other hand, changes in family structures may provide an impetus for work-at-home projects). The costs and benefits to both employees and employers are varied. Work-at-home benefits from the organization's viewpoint include: reduced travel and energy costs, the ability to attract and retain otherwise unattainable people, improved motivation and productivity, reduced turnover, off-hour utilization of the computer, and reduced overhead.

The disadvantages associated with working at home from an organization viewpoint include: less management control of the work environment and productivity, communications problems, and social issues such as the worker's increased independence from the employer, or reduced identification with the corporation.

For employees, the advantages of working home can include less time and money spent commuting, more time for family life, flexibility of work schedule, loose supervision, an increased feeling of community and reduced clothing costs. Potential problems include social isolation, lack of clerical support, reduced image/status in the organization and higher home energy costs. Working at home can reorient the home around the needs of the business, and so affect the lives of the spouses and children. Some may enjoy the new orientation, some may resent it.

One of the most difficult aspects of implementing alternative work-site programs is the difficulty for employees in adjusting to remote management. Therefore, in planning such programs, management needs to choose the right individuals and the right jobs. Employees who work independently and are self-motivated are better candidates and participation should be voluntary. Management should cultivate a climate of mutual respect and trust. There should be open lines of communication and clearly defined results. Finally, the long-term expectations and consequences of these programs should be determined in advance. In particular, long-term career paths will be of concern to both employee and employer. Employees must not fear that they are disappearing from view. Salary, benefits and insurance coverage need to be carefully considered.

Do work-at-home programs really work? Early experiences have indicated that there is some potential. For example, Control Data started a program a number of years ago to re-train disabled employees to do computer-based work at their homes, resulting in reduced costs and providing work to those who may not otherwise be able to do so. After a year of operating the program, called Homework, Control Data found that the productivity of the worker had improved. The improvement was a result of reduced travel time to work. By working at home, or close by, employee motivation had increased. The previously-mentioned need for social contact has resulted in an underground computer-based gossip channel.

At Trigon Systems Group, employees have the option of working at home, particularly when working on major reports or development programs. But to be honest, we've had some problems. For example, it's 2 a.m. and one of us is working on a chapter of this book due to go to the editor first thing in the morning. The system goes down. It's the middle of December and the temperature is minus 10 Celsius. The choice is to get in the car and drive to the office to bring the system back up, or crawl into a nice warm bed and go into the office early in the morning to finish it. What do you do? You crawl into bed, feeling somewhat guilty. While such support considerations should be carefully accounted for in the design of work-at-home programs, there will always be times such as this. Expect them.

A Strategy for the Work Environment

This chapter deals with the *settings* in which people work. As the enterprise is transformed through its use of the new technology, planning is required to enable appropriate changes to the physical plant and work environment. Part of the process of strategic planning for integrated systems is to lay out policies and plans regarding the office environment. This component of the three main architectures of office systems is highlighted in Figure 12.1.

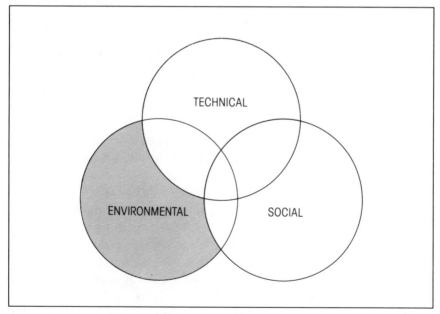

Figure 12.1   Environment: The Third Architecture

As mentioned earlier, to the classic Greeks architecture was an expression of values. Taken from today's viewpoint, the environmental aspects of office automation deal with designing workplaces which meet both the mission and goals of the organization as well as the human and social needs of the persons occupying the space. The alignment of the environmental with the human and technological design of the integrated office is necessary to maximize the performance of the work system.

Traditionally, it has been easy to measure the costs of walls, desks and other office furnishings. On the other hand, office productivity has remained hard to quantify. At the same time, cost-effectiveness formulas for workspace design have traditionally emphasized the costs while paying little attention to human effectiveness. As a result, officeworkers and their companies as a whole have generally been shortchanged by poorly conceived environmental designs.

Paying attention to the ergonomic factors can have a high payoff in terms of employee motivation, morale and productivity. To understand these factors you must look at the tasks employees perform and the overall management of the tasks, the architectural location of the task and the workstation design.

Why is the office environment so ill-equipped to handle the introduction of this new technology? Well, from an historical viewpoint, there has been little change in the manner in which an office functions over the last one hundred years. Until recently the primary concern of the office was the movement of paper-based information. The introduction of the integrated office has shifted the focus to the display terminal. Information is now being input through a keyboard (or possibly by voice), and the input is read through a raised, vertical reflective screen covered with glowing figures. This simple change has resulted in space planning problems as well as concerns for health and safety.

Consider a typical example of the problems facing organizations implementing an integrated office. A large manufacturing organization moved its marketing group to a new office in a high-rise office tower. While initial impressions of the new office design were favorable, the introduction of computer and telecommunications equipment quickly revealed the lack of foresight in the building and office planning process.

The first problem arose when the phone company attempted to install a new private branch exchange (PBX) for telecommunications. It was quickly discovered that the architects had not left enough room for such equipment in the central locations normally allocated. Further problems developed when terminals were introduced into the workstations. The introduction of the integrated office meant redesigning the jobs of both the administrative staff and professional staff. As a result, reporting relationships were altered, job descriptions changed, procedures and workflow patterns altered. The workstation and relationships of the original office plan no longer made sense and because the office plan was relatively fixed, it was very difficult to reorganize the office to reflect the new reporting relationships.

The introduction of the terminals immediately produced problems of glare from the fluorescent lighting. Where possible, workstations were rearranged in an attempt to reduce the glare. In other cases, shields had to be fitted over the fluorescent lighting in order to gain significant improvements. The lesson here is that superficial impressions can ignore a Pandora's box of potential problems.

---

1. Computer room in the wrong place.
2. Too few electrical outlets.
3. Outdated fluorescent lighting.
4. Printers used in working areas without proper sound insulation.
5. Terminals that don't meet ergonomic standards.
6. Terminals used on traditional office furniture.
7. Chairs that don't support body – but do tip over.
8. Inattention to cable requirements.
9. People in the wrong place.
10. Thinking in square feet when people work in three dimensions.

Figure 12.2   Ten Common Mistakes

Many organizations implementing their first integrated office system into an already existing environment face a significant and immediate problem — how to wire the system. In older buildings, stringing coaxial cable can be difficult if not impossible. In one case, that of a new building, the cost of cabling was going to be $22 million because the builder did not have the foresight to include flexibility for such wiring as the building was being constructed. Novel wiring methods, such as flat wires buried under carpeting, are helping to alleviate some of these problems. New, wireless methods of transmitting information in local areas can also be anticipated. The use of infrared light links and cellular radio are examples.

As a final example of poor environmental/ergonomic planning, the introduction of a newly automated system for telephone operators in one telephone company created numerous problems for the operators. First, the operators were moved from several very large cord-equipped board offices to modern decentralized offices, which were usually as close to their homes as possible. This was seen as a desirable move by the operators. However, the physical designs of the new offices created a number of problems, the most acute of which was produced by light reflecting from the windows onto the terminal screens. While the windows were a much desired change for the operators, the often intense natural light, improperly shielded, resulted in eye strain. Second, the operators' workstations were designed for the "average" operator. There was little, if any, flexibility to change the position of the screen, keyboard or desk.

At the same time, each operator was given her or his own private workspace, a U-shaped desk with side panels. Because the operators came from an environment where there was high visual access to the office operations, many now felt cut off from their peers. Finally, there was little flexibility in the manner in which the operator worked at the workstation. Standing for other than a moment was prohibited by most supervisors in most offices, as it was said to decrease productivity. The workstation was designed for operation from the sitting position only, yet most of us would agree that it is difficult to sit for six hours a day. Office workers must have the freedom to stand or move about the office.

Multi-level Office Planning

For purposes of organizational planning, we can divide the environmental planning requirements into three levels: corporate level, departmental or divisional level, and individual. These three levels of planning are illustrated in Figure 12.3.

At the corporate level, the policy focus is on providing direction for the architects and engineers who determine the building site, and the overall exterior and interior design. The individual level is the domain of the interior designer or space planner and the focus is on the individual workspace, with the end-users often not even consulted about their requirements. It is at the mid-level, the department, where there is concern over shared spaces, that various combinations of architects, engineers, space planners and interior designers may wish to exert their influence. Indeed, the lack of an integrated approach is most evident at this level.

While consideration must be given to simply physical factors, attention should also be focused on the psychological factors which are important for each of the three levels. For example, at the corporate level, the size, shape, materials and overall design of the building will say much about the cultural values of the organization. At the departmental level, spatial relationships will either facilitate or curtail communications between employees. And at the individual level, the space and furniture allocated to each employee in relation to other employees will affect their well being.

Many studies have shown a need for employees to possess a defined space. A violation of this space can result in real physical discomfort.

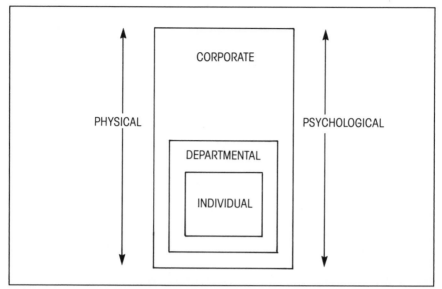

Figure 12.3 Levels of Office Planning

Humans use boundaries to define their territories, and while such boundaries do not necessarily provide legal right, they do provide proprietary right. Violation of the boundary may result in anger, a feeling of loss and a desire to regain the space. Providing proper settings will encourage people to do work worthy of that setting. Attractive meeting places can make people feel comfortable and important. Neutral locations which preclude territorial problems will encourage participants to bring strength and individuality to the task. Flexible seating arrangements will encourage people to establish their own spaces.

In a sense, we are witnessing a convergence of space planning responsibilities, just as we have witnessed the convergence of data processing, communications and the office technologies. Figure 12.4 illustrates this convergence.

We are beginning to see the use of coalitions to facilitate a comprehensive design process. At the same time, new approaches to building design are focusing on the user as designer. Architects and designers are working with end-users to literally build from the inside out, taking into careful consideration the functional, physical and psychological requirements.

Environmental Planning at the Corporate Level

Building facilities include devices or features that are either a part of the building or attached to it, which encourage convenient and efficient use

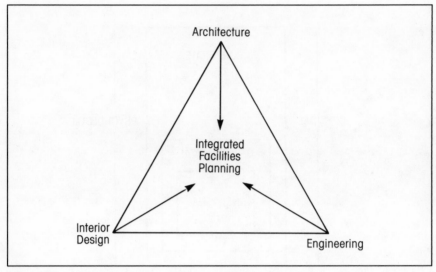

Figure 12.4 Converging Space Planning Responsibilities

of space. This also includes common areas and services such as the halls, stairways, air conditioning, fire protection and other fixed features.

Planners of new systems generally fall into two groups: those organizations planning to build *new* facilities of which the integrated office will be a part and those organizations in *existing* buildings where such systems are already being implemented.

In the case of a new building there is an opportunity to plan for the needs of all departments — communications, administration and data processing. Ensuring adequate conduits for either coaxial or fiber optic cabling should be high on the list of considerations.

Traditionally, there were separate runways for low voltage telephone and communications systems and high voltage electrical current. As a result many older buildings are substandard for today's wiring needs, necessitating either new conduits on the floor surface or some other alternative to bring the wiring up to standard. In many new buildings, cellular steel subfloors buried in the concrete floors provide connections which are never more than a few feet from the desired location.

Consideration must also be given to which type of local area network might be employed. If the PBX is to be used as the medium to switch both voice and data traffic, the wiring may be considerably less expensive, as twisted pair wires may suffice.

Another issue to be resolved is the location of special rooms for central computers — mainframes, minicomputers, or super-microcomputers — and their specialized wiring and air-conditioning requirements. Large corporations still rely very much on large mainframes for much of their heavy data processing, but these may often be located at another site. In such cases, it is necessary to ensure high speed data links between locations.

While the older models of minicomputers still require special air-conditioning, newer models do not and may therefore be located within a user department. However, they still throw considerable heat, and require fans for cooling. When minis are combined with numerous terminals located in a department, consideration should be given to additional cooling vents and sources of electrical power. In particular, special power lines may be required to ensure that common building fluctuations do not disrupt service. This is particularly important when users are working from remote locations, outside of normal office hours.

The integrated office is different from the data-processing environment in that once a user becomes familiar with the system, there is an expectation that it will be available twenty-four-hours-a-day, seven-days-a-week. This means careful planning of routine system maintenance and back-up.

In the design process, the organization has a responsibility to set standards related to specific organization functions. These include services performed, unique workflow requirements and technical aids which facilitate management support. As well, design should reflect the mission and goals of the organization, especially the type of work atmosphere desired.

In its corporate policy regarding the work environment, one organization set the following general standards: all comparable functions within the organization should have similar workstation designs, standardized furniture systems should be used throughout the organization, and all work areas will use open concept planning with no full height partitions.

While the setting of standards is asserting a degree of control over people, it means that future reorganization is facilitated because all components are standardized. Once the policy is set, it is possible to develop a set of procedures with a common glossary of terms.

For aesthetic reasons, the corporation at large should have the responsibility for setting standards for the purchase of office equipment such as desks, chairs, and dividing units. The range of color should also be set at this level.

The corporation will also be responsible for maintaining proper temperature, humidity and ventilation for the building. Most often, the office temperature is too high, resulting in drowsiness and discomfort. Improper ventilation has similar results. Humidity also has an impact on the comfort and efficiency of the human being. Given the same temperature, moist air will feel warm and dry air cool. Too much humidity may result in physical discomfort of a respiratory nature and induce a heavy, languid feeling. On the other hand, excessive dryness can make people feel parched and irritable.

Environmental Planning at the Departmental Level

Depending on the size of the department, the degree of autonomy from corporate policy as a whole may vary significantly. In small to medium size organizations, the responsibility for office planning and design is likely to remain at the corporate level. However, in large organizations, this may not be the case, especially when departments are located in different physical structures.

Planning at the departmental level should focus on the interrelationships between the various work groups within the department. This will mean very careful planning of the physical space, with due consideration to the tasks performed and the resultant flow of information. Understanding how the space is to be used and the movement of people in it (known as *proxemics*) can help to improve the quality of communications, level of comfort, and overall productivity.

Placement of office furniture can communicate a degree of formality or informality. For example, chairs behind desks create barriers and foster short, formal interactions. Eliminating the barrier helps to relax the atmosphere and encourages longer and more open interaction.

In the case of a northwestern U.S. construction company, the office design was determined very much by the attitude of the president, who recognized the need for both the physical and visual levels of communications. The office was developed as a horizontal concept, completely open. All personnel including the president are in view of each other. The electronic office systems are connected through conduits running throughout the office at desk level rather than in subfloor raceways. All communication in the office, as symbolized by this integral design, is completely open. and everyone in the office can see each other. In essence, the entire area has become staff space in an attempt to compensate for the alienation individual workstations may potentially bring about.

Environmental Planning at the Individual Level

It may also make sense to provide information, formulate guidelines or even policies regarding critical issues which have a direct impact on the individual and the setting within which he or she works.

Although there are numerous studies demonstrating that architecture and physical layout can substantially influence variables such as patterns of communication and social interaction, there is little information on the impact the physical characteristics of a work organization may have on outcomes such as employee satisfaction and productivity, which are relevant to employee and organizational health.

The physical context of an organization does have its influence on employee's work. The absence of physical boundaries in a workspace (the open concept) creates experiences for employees which differ substantially from those they encounter if working in an area bounded by walls or partitions.

Physical boundaries can influence employee job experiences in two ways. First, boundaries can transform a work area into a space which is defensible. A bounded work area provides the opportunity for privacy and hence personal conversations and the sharing of information. At the same time the number of interruptions may be reduced. Second, a divided area helps to clarify the nature of the work process, so that tasks are more easily identified as well as the equipment to complete those tasks.

An office system must be designed in the context of the jobs to be done, and its context must take into account such factors as autonomy, task identity, supervisor and co-worker feedback, opportunity for friendship, ability to concentrate, skill variety, task significance and task feedback. These aspects of good job design are highly relevant to the design of office systems which provide a balance of the technical and social components. For example, some believe that an open layout limits possibilities for interaction, leading to to decreases in task identity, friendship opportunities, and supervisor and co-worker feedback. As these variables relate to employee satisfaction, motivation, and productivity, the open-office concept might be expected to lead to reduce the amount of work completed.

What appears to be emerging is a new discipline integrating facilities' requirements with the overall strategic plan of the organization. This new discipline has been entitled "space management".[1]

As mentioned earlier, introduction of the computer terminal has brought about a fundamental change in information handling within the office. People are now required to input information via a keyboard and to read it from a screen. As a result, new problems have arisen in the design of work environments.

A comprehensive overview of the related issues has been prepared by Professor Olaf Ustber of Lulea University, Sweden, in *The VDT Manual*. A further comprehensive bibliography is available from Dr. Marvin Dainoff, Department of Psychology, Miami University, Oxford, Ohio. In addition, the work of W.O. Galitz and Sabine Rohlfs have provided sources for some of the information which follows.

While planners should not attempt to design each individual workstation, they should come to grips with all common requirements. Necessary background for the overall design process will include an understanding of job procedures and workflow, communications, existing general attitudes towards the new systems, and knowledge of the physical design features of the new system components and the functions to which they will be put. Other considerations will be the office environment factors that exist in the workspace of a person and affect productivity, such as lighting, acoustics, temperature, and workstation design.

An effective office design will concentrate on three fundamental perspectives of the user: needs, characteristics, and expectations. Needs include both basic human needs and job requirements. These will be discussed in further detail later in this chapter. Characteristics include the areas of sensations, attention, memory, and cognition. The user interface must be consistent with user expectations and viewed with acceptance. Finally, user expectations are probably the most critical influence in the user's overall reaction to new systems. Expectations based on other available technologies (such as the typewriter) will likely have been high, thereby requiring any new technology to behave in a predictable, reliable and responsive manner.

Lighting

Perhaps the most obvious problem, and the one easiest to deal with, is office lighting. Improper lighting conditions can either entirely obliterate the image on the screen or significantly reduce the contrast ratio.

Proper lighting has two basic qualities. It must be of a sufficient level to fulfill the needs of the person doing the work and it must produce minimal glare. Reduction of glare is possible through a number of alternatives. The first is indirect lighting, which may almost totally eliminate the undesired imaging of the light source on the tube. A second option, one more common with lower ceiling heights (nine feet or less), is the attachment to the light fixture of some type of lens in the "parawedge" family. A third possibility is the use of anti-reflection filters. However, while the use of a micro-mesh filter will subdue the reflection/glare condition, the sacrifice is a reduction in both contrast ratio and image intensity. The general trend is towards the elimination of all direct overhead lighting, such as fluorescent lights, substituting ambient or task lighting.

Placement of the furniture also plays a part in the total equation. For example, facing a screen to an improperly treated window will cause problems. Windows must be properly shaded and the screen set at an appropriate angle from them.

Acoustical Requirements

Perhaps the single most important element in the overall design is the need to provide for aural privacy. In a study by Steelcase/Louis Harris "the ability to concentrate without noise and other distractions" was rated by respondents as the most important item when it came to doing their job well.[2] The degree to which users will accept and be effective within an open office plan depends very much on the degree of speech privacy and control of distracting noise provided at each workplace. The two key concepts are background noise, often fairly constant in level, and activity noise, which must be reduced in many cases.

The introduction of new office systems is accompanied by the sounds of keyboards, printers and, even possibly, the computer. Printer sound can be reduced by sound covers. Sounds from the terminal keyboard can be reduced or even eliminated, although the feedback from the keys is preferred by many people.

Looking into the future, the importance of voice input to systems will undoubtedly increase as the technology matures, and this may create new noise problems for office design. People will probably be talking more than they normally do today, (for example, on the telephone), thereby adding to the overall level of noise. It may be that people will prefer to speak when inputting text or messages because it is easier. However, they may wish to read replies because reading is easier than listening. Compression techniques which leave messages intelligible to the human ear are possible, but whether they will be acceptable to the average user is unknown. Also, the retention span for spoken material tends to be shorter than for written text.

As with lighting, acoustical standards can be determined by current industry norms. It is possible to measure noise levels in individual offices by using a noise meter. Sound levels above 60 decibels in an office are considered noisy. High noise levels can affect both the physiological and psychological well-being of personnel, with typical symptoms being increased blood pressure, increased muscular tension, increased heart rate, general tension, mental stress, and the inability to think and work properly.

Any sound usually competes for a person's attention. If the sound is unpleasant, it will be considered as noise. As people are a major source of noise in an office, it is important that the conversations of other people not be understood. That is, an awareness of conversation may be acceptable, but not of the content.

A well-planned office means that sound and noise levels are maintained at levels that eliminate distractions, provide for good hearing and speech privacy. In planning an office, the primary objective is to minimize to the greatest degree possible sound-reflective surfaces so that sounds diminish quickly according to the laws of physics (about six decibels per doubling of distance). An effective noise control program should focus on three areas: the use of efficient sound-absorbing materials, a masking sound system, and office layout.

Workstation Requirements

A final component of the office environment plan is the proper arrangement and design of the workstations. Over the past decade, the trend has been to more open office plans — a large work area functionally organized and landscaped with trees, plants and possibly dividers. Presumed benefits of such arrangements are economy, better lighting, acoustics and climate. There are also organizational benefits, such as quicker communication of information and ease of reorganization. On the other hand, there are strong arguments against open plans: psychosocial factors such as visual and auditory distractions, and lower motivation.

The key concept in the design of the workplace is to approach it from the point of view of human performance effectiveness. The design should therefore proceed from a detailed task analysis. A clear definition is required of all operational requirements, the functions that have to be performed, the sequence of operations, and the flow of information required to accomplish the tasks in a timely manner. The end product of this analysis should be a set of specifications which will describe needed workstation components and how these components might interrelate.

The human needs that might be applied to the workstation design range from those which are biological (bodily, sensory) to those which are psychological in nature (social, motivational, aesthetic).

Workstations should be designed to allow the user the greatest economy of effort. Such factors as sitting or standing heights, reach lengths, arm angles in keying, and eye viewing angles all contribute to the comfort of performing necessary office tasks. Poor workstation design will ultimately result in fatigue, more errors and slower task performance.

Sensory factors are also important, in particular sight and hearing. For example, the directional nature of sight has implications for the location of displays and visual signals. Legibility and eye convergence requirements impose limits for positioning source documents or display screens. The non-directional nature of hearing has implications for the location of auditory signals. Ambient factors such as temperature and humidity are often out of the control of the user and therefore require special attention at the department or corporate level.

Developing a positive attitude towards work requires satisfying the need for privacy, individuality, status and belonging. Privacy means having the ability to engage in conversations requiring security or confidentiality; freedom from being interrupted while concentrating or performing creative work; and protection from unwanted noises or sounds.

Good workstation design depends upon the proper construction of the parts as well as the ultimate configuration. Compromises may be necessary in design, but workstations should be constructed considering what is best for the user.

The most significant new component of the workstation is the video display unit. Most often VDTs are introduced in the office with little concern about the best viewing conditions or the best operating conditions. The end result is that the user experiences extreme physical discomfort.

The introduction of the VDT has also been accompanied by rising fears of their potential hazard to the users' health. Initial concerns were primarily about radiation, but more recently this has expanded to include *psychological* and *physiological* side effects such as vision and muscle or skeletal problems.

Perhaps the most direct way to help avoid extensive psychological discomfort is to involve the users in the design of the system. This input can help alleviate health fears, stress and fears of job loss. Most people fear change and if they cannot express this feeling openly they may indeed become sick. It is important that employees understand their role in the work process, have a sense of control over their tasks, and appreciate the importance of their jobs, if they are not to be isolated in their work environment.

Radiation

The issue of health hazards in office automation is a hotly debated topic in North America. By way of contrast, in Scandinavia it is automatically assumed that office automation presents hazards to users' health and the issue is how to eliminate them.

There is a considerable body of literature on the issue of radiation resulting from the introduction of VDTs. There are in fact two types of electromagnetic radiation energy, ionizing and non-ionizing, with the former having a greater damaging capacity. Numerous studies have failed to detect ionizing radiation from video display terminals above natural background levels.

While today's evidence suggests that radiation emission from VDTs is low and does not constitute a health hazard, there is much concern over the long-term effects of low level radiation from many sources, including VDTs. Additional research will help to resolve some of the these issues. It may be appropriate to adopt a corporate policy regarding periodic testing for malfunctioning VDTs which emit radiation above the safety limits.

Fatigue

Fatigue caused by VDTs is thought to result primarily from sustained effort to see the screen clearly and maintain a fixed posture at the keyboard. Extended visual attention to detail with little eye movement, along with potentially little auditory stimulation, can lead to fatigue and eyestrain. Prolonged stationary postures will similarly result in generalized fatigue, because the body is designed for movement.

It is therefore important that planned periods away from the VDT be built into jobs which require prolonged working in front of a screen. This may be more applicable to clerical personnel as the multi-task nature of most white collar jobs helps to ensure that people are not in front of terminals for periods of more than a few hours. Also, these people normally have the freedom to take the required breaks when and if they desire.

Vision

For viewing distances of under twenty feet, one-third of the focusing ability is carried out by the internal muscles of the eye and by the elasticity of the lens. The remaining two-thirds is carried out by the cornea and internal fluids of the eye.

Normally, the internal and external muscles do not normally become fatigued or exhausted. It is possible however to develop eye fatigue from a prolonged effort to see clearly, because visual acuity is not a fixed property of the eye but a function that depends on visual capacity, as well as on the level of illumination, color, glare, contrast, and character size.

Sometime between the ages of twenty and sixty the focusing capacity tends to be reduced by up to 25 percent as the lens becomes less flexible. The consequence is a slower ability to accommodate distances, a diminished ability to detect small differences in light levels, and increased sensitivity to glare. These changes must be taken into consideration when designing work environments.

Because visual acuity is so important in the performance of work related to the integrated office, special attention should be paid to the quality of the VDT display image. The resolution of the display image is determined by the character size and the spacing between the characters. If the characters are too small or close together, legibility is reduced. If the characters are too large, the result is that the phosphor dots appear to dissociate.

Common VDT problems include flicker, screen movement caused by power fluctuations, decreased clarity, and brightness as a result of grime on the screen or deteriorating cathode ray tubes. The latter problems can be fixed by periodic screen cleaning and replacing of old tubes. The former problems can be avoided by ensuring a proper flicker rate (60 Hertz or cycles per second) or by using dedicated power lines.

Viewing problems can be lessened by a more viewable display, such as an orange-phosphor cathode ray tube (CRT), which displays a yellow text on an amber background. This brighter primary viewing area reduces contrast glare and the need for eye adaptations, as yellow is at the top of the visual sensitivity curve and less brightness is needed to perceive it. The orange screen appears to be the preferred color of VDT users. [3]

Poorly designed workplaces can lead to posture problems and muscle tension. Proper seating is a must, or the result will be fatigue in calf, thigh, back and neck muscles. Chairs should be adjustable from a seated position, stable (five legs on casters), have no arm rests to interfere with arm movements, have a bi-directionally adjustable backrest to support the spine and lumbar region. They should also have a rounded seat front to avoid cutting into the thighs, flexible upholstered material to distribute sitting, and woven covering to prevent slippage, body heat buildup and perspiration. Foot rests may be necessary for some operators.

Desks should provide sufficient space for documents, and other working items, adequate legroom, and proper thickness to maintain correct arm position. Keyboards should be detached and of minimum thickness to ensure correct elevation. Placement of document holders next to the screen at the proper angle, distance and height helps to minimize eye adjustments and reflected glare from the source document. Proper attention must also be paid to the arms, head, spine, pelvis, abdomen and thighs of the seated operator.

New Sensibilities

This chapter, will close with a reference to a concept put forth by Naisbitt in *Megatrends* — the notion of the high tech/high touch environment.

He claims that whenever there is new technology introduced into the environment there is a counterbalancing human response of high touch. Without the high touch the concept is rejected. And the more high tech the more high touch.

When there is dissonance created as a result of the introduction of high tech, problems result. Say, for example, you call a friend to leave a message and are answered with "Hi, I'm not available to talk to you right now, but if you would like to leave your name and telephone number . . .". The response in many cases is to hang-up immediately or to leave some meaningless message.

The introduction of high tech into the office should therefore mean that people will want to spend more time together, just meeting, or "schmoozing". Thus, it is likely that people will want to continue to go to the office as a place of work and that the concept of the electronic cottage as a workplace for the majority of officeworkers may be somewhat off the mark. What is clear, is that the new technology must be balanced with an environment which provides the opportunity for self-fulfillment and personal growth. An initial planning document, discussing the environmental implications and proposing such new initial policies is a good way to start.

A Strategy for Leading Change

Change of the scope precipitated by integrated technologies itself requires a senior management strategy implemented through policies, processes, and in general, leadership.

Change can be considered as the process of creating something which does not currently exist. It involves bringing the desired into the present. Change involves people letting go of what is, to enable what is desired. To lead this process you will have to create the conditions where ongoing change is accepted as a way of life.

A theme of this book is that technology profoundly affects people, their jobs and relationships with one another, the organizational context within which people achieve objectives, and the very nature of the business itself. "Transitioning" of this scope requires leadership to provide the motivation for change and movement. Leading such change — the transition from "where we are" to "where we want to be" — requires identification of the conditions for successful movement.

This approach is quite at variance with many traditional approaches to implementing or "installing" (as the word is used) technology. Often word processors were plunked on the desktop of the new user or parachuted into the workgroup with little involvement or preparation of the individual for the changes to take place. Often, it was not necessary. New telephone systems required minimal involvement by users because of the simplicity of the technology. Data-processing terminals were generally used by a limited number of technically knowledgeable individuals so the problem of managing change was not sharply posed.

With the advent of the corporate micro as part of an integrated office system, the situation is quite different. For the first time everyone in the office is a potential user of an electronic workstation. To this situation people throughout the organization bring their hopes, expectations, fears, insecurities and desires for involvement and participation in the transformation of their working lives. This calls for leadership, and leaders.

The starting point for successful leadership is to ensure that the change, rather than being injurious to the potential users, will be of real and actual benefit to the individual. If a system plan will improve the quality of work life of the individuals involved, the challenge of leading change is quite different than for a plan which will result in a deterioration in the quality of their working experience. In the former case, the challenge is one of soliciting involvement and cooperation in a process which is in the interests of the individual. In the latter, the challenge is to manipulate people into acting against their own self interest.

Transitioning also requires the fostering of a process wherein people can participate fully and reap the benefits of change. This includes the development of a climate of acceptance through policies which encourage education and the implementation of corporate-wide awareness programs. Through such programs, misconceptions can be overcome and an understanding of the desired state achieved. Once this understanding has been gained, people will require training in the necessary skills to enable movement. Finally, movement can take place through a defined action plan which will bring together all the activities, resources, investments and schedules required for successful implementation of systems and planning.

Leadership

The term "leadership", rather than "management", better describes the key requirement for successful change. To begin, there is more involved than the "good management" of a routine process where approaches are well-documented, with outcomes that are fairly predictable because of prior experience with the degree of change these systems bring about. Instead, we are dealing with innovation on a wide scale with which only a handful of enterprises and individuals have had actual experience. The implementation and change process that these systems require has not been well chronicled. Although the failure literature is considerable, there is little guidance as to the right approach to leading an innovation of this scope. In general, we are breaking new ground; forging new concepts of what works best.

Moreover, we are moving into a period where traditional "management" approaches of using power *over people* to achieve results, is changing to the concept of "leadership", where power *with people* to achieve results is needed. This shift has been precipitated, in part, by a new desire on the part of workers for more control and self-management of jobs, work content and career development. Such independence of thought and action by workers or users has been accompanied by the desire for more participation in deriving positive outcomes that are beneficial to the enterprise and to the individual. The unplanned proliferation of micros is an example of how users are seeking and finding their own way to satisfy their needs for tools to assist in their work and to be successful in their jobs.

However, if a dictatorial management style is inappropriate, so is anarchy. If systems installations are proceeding on an unplanned route, wandering aimlessly through the labyrinth of implementation and other issues, neither the corporate goals nor the needs of the individual can be met. Clearly there is a need for leadership.

The individual or individuals who will provide leadership should be knowledgeable in the significant aspects of introducing these systems. We have found that a system implementor or planner must be perceived to have "earned the right" to lead this type of process. This does not mean that the leader must have a sophisticated knowledge of technology, but rather must be aware of the potential the technology provides and its limitations. Maintaining the right to lead means, among other things, staying on top of the process; exhibiting insight when confronted with problems; giving directions that are consistent with existing plans, and knowing when to be flexible in making necessary changes to strategy.

Leadership requires openness to ideas; people need to feel they are able to influence an established policy or procedure if the case is well made. Setting goals for people, within a reasonable expectation level, with built-in measures of performance and feedback, will instill confidence in the leadership of that process.

The art of leading systems planning and implementations is often an acquired one. Take the issue of visibility. It is important that management be very visible during a period of high change and movement, and when there is little movement, available for consultation and advice. A good leader must be able to think as a helicopter moves. This means having the ability to move from the detail of individual tasks and issues to a view of the whole picture or organizational context in order to give effective direction. In summary, leadership is required to motivate people to accept change and to participate positively in the transition.

It may make sense, as part of a strategic plan for integrated office systems, to adopt policies and programs to encourage leadership of change. These can include involvement of end-users in the process of change; support for multi-disciplinary project teams and rewards for those leading successful implementations. Leadership workshops and seminars can be organized to promote the new approaches to management of change.

Transitioning Strategy

Leadership, whether in winning football games or improving organizational performance, requires strategy. Among other things, a transition strategy, as shown in Figure 13.1, should:

- Identify the conditions for successful movement
- Carefully time the introduction of change
- Plan for shifts in roles and responsibilities

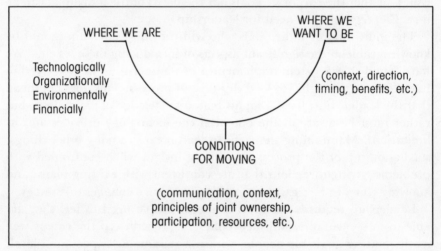

Figure 13.1 Transitioning Strategy

This requires some rethinking of our past "installation" mentality where things were supposed to be transformed overnight. The diffusion of an innovation of this character takes years, even decades. In a sense we have moved into a period of ongoing transition. New ideas spring forth and the demand for change increases as people become involved in the transition. We have seen this occur in settings where joint ownership and commitment to change are developed between the implementor and user. Responsibility is shared equally with risk; it is no longer the implementor alone who shoulders the burden of change, rather the user working with the implementor.

Building such a joint ownership plan requires that you:

- Identify those whose commitment is essential (the opinion leaders in the organization)
- Secure their support and involvement so that they get past their own alarms, and go into the implementation process as experimenters and critics who are constantly trying to make the project work

- Communicate the rewards and success derived from the project to motivate others to want to change as well.

Creating the Climate for Change

There is a set of conditions essential for successful change of this type. The individual needs the ability to "actualize" or manage the job relative to his or her lifestyle expectations and constraints, assuming responsibility for the outcome. A set of "liberating" conditions define the job content and scope. The "enabling" conditions then require review and appraisal, ensuring that those necessary are provided or planned for in order that the individual can manage job context. Finally, the "integrating" conditions need to be defined and communicated, providing the individual with the organizational context, mission, and goals to be achieved, along with solid leadership.

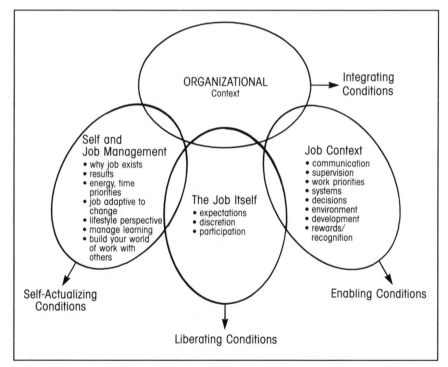

Figure 13.2   Creating Conditions for Change

As such conditions are established, movement can take place (Figure 13.2). But how much movement is desirable, acceptable, manageable?

Determining the appropriate timing for initiation of a strategic planning effort or a pilot implementation is a judgment call that involves

testing the "water" to see if the temperature is right. Education and awareness sessions may be required to provide people with information that
will help them understand the nature of the change involved, and what is
possible with the help of technology.

Changing Roles and Responsibilities

As the nature of systems change, encompassing new technologies, new
users and new approaches, so must the roles and responsibilities of those
who implement, and those who use these systems. As an organization
evolves in its use of technology, the nature of the work involved in implementing systems changes and the degree of involvement shifts from the
systems professional to the user. Several themes emerge:

- User management will need help in assuming a responsible role in the
  implementation process, and be made aware of how their individual
  work system contributes to and is supported by the enterprise system.
- The Human Resources group will need to be involved more and more
  as these roles and responsibilities evolve, with skills in organizational
  development and job redesign.
- The role of the implementor will shift from individual work group and
  departmental systems implementation to enterprise systems management and evolution. This role could involve coordination across user
  groups to communicate cross-functional ideas and issues, to facilitate
  the use of systems and to educate user groups as to new technology
  trends and advanced applications.
- The user will have greater freedom to develop individual, work group
  and departmental systems as need dictates, with decisionmaking autonomy over acquisitions and realization of benefits.
- Leadership may initially be provided by an "innovator", or someone
  who has the courage, foresight and power to influence change. As acceptance of these new concepts is gained, the leadership may change
  to a more formalized functional group, where all systems responsibilities converge with the integration of the various components.
- As mentioned earlier, steering committees, coalitions of and other ad
  hoc groupings are critical in the initiation period. As integrated office
  systems are consolidated, more permanent structures arise.

Creating a Learning Environment

Howard Organ, an American office automation consultant, explains the
difference between training and education as follows: "For my twelve year

old daughter, sex education is okay, but training is out." Successful transitioning and the leadership of change require both. As part of a plan, it makes sense to formulate strategies to *educate* the people in your organization — equipping them with key concepts — and to *train* them how to use the new technology. Both efforts can be part of creating a "learning environment" in which the human resource has access to the knowledge and skills necessary for high performance and quality of work life.

Education Strategies

Through education, an understanding of the purpose of the change can be attained, connecting the vision of what will be to the changes being implemented. Further, education should provide knowledge of what each person's contribution will be.

It is critical to communicate a common perspective on how the technology will be applied. People should understand how systems will be used, what the system will provide, how they will be able to use it effectively, and what changes to workflow, procedures, jobs and relationships will be required. There should be a feeling of confidence that the system will actually deliver and a sense of ownership that opportunities for "hands on" and self-directed learning help create.

In the experiments we have conducted in offices through the years, we have identified a correlation between an individual's conceptual knowledge of what the system is (ultimately) capable of and the actual extent of use. It seems that those who understand what is possible can develop abilities far beyond the initial training concepts.

Corporate policies, guidelines and information — as part of a plan — can be very useful in standardizing the quality of education and helping the organization as a whole move towards a learning environment.

A learning environment should be free from threat and judgment so that people can go beyond their fears to openly embrace the system and begin to adopt it into their daily working lives. An ongoing strategy to communicate and educate people at all levels within the organization as to progress, new trends in technology, successful implementations, concepts of managing change, ideas for new approaches and applications, and overall plans, is essential for successful movement.

Training Strategies

Those affected by change will also require training in the skills and competencies necessary to move the organization to the desired state that is its goal. This is the area for which many organizations new to implementing integrated systems fail to adequately plan. Training, as delivered by suppliers, is quite narrowly defined as providing the information necessary to know which button to push to create a given outcome.

For this reason, corporate policies, as part of a plan, are needed to ensure high quality training and at the same time improve the efficiency by which users acquire the skills and competencies required for the changing nature of work.

From our experience, training requirements are grossly underestimated. The cost of training, the time required and the skills needed to provide effective training are often overlooked until after systems have been in place for some time, and the amount of troubleshooting and support have skyrocketed.

Traditional word-processing systems could be learned in a few days if the system was stand-alone. Several months may be required for integrated systems with shared facilities and multiple functions including communications, decision support, and information and administrative tools.

Besides the complexity of the system, training schemes must also be flexible enough to accommodate a number of personal attributes, such as general aptitude and previous experience. Former determinants such as age may be less relevant than the person's attitude towards change. Given the right setting and program for training, there is no reason older workers cannot learn how to use the new technologies. However, any employee, regardless of age, who finds the training too difficult or stressful, should be given alternatives within the organization.

Unnecessary stress is often caused by having left the decisions about whom, how and when to train up to the vendor. No training scheme should be approved unless it has been tested and found to meet the organization's overall criteria for implementation. There's little sense in having a systems design which respects the needs of the employees if the training program does not. Consider the effect of a training procedure that uses a piercing screech to tell the work system user that he or she has done something wrong — and the only way to turn the horrible noise off is to correct the mistake. Imagine how frantic you would become if nothing worked. Such training procedures actually exist. The tragedy is that they can be so easily avoided if someone first tries them out.

Timing is another important decision. While it may be tempting to "get it over with", you really can't. Training programs must evolve in conjunction with the new work systems. There is little benefit in training people to use equipment that is not yet available.

In organizations which have a great number of suppliers, the problem of training is more acute. The group which is responsible for training will need to be aware of many different training packages, what is necessary to support these systems, and of systems upgrades requiring retraining.

During an organization's planning for integrated office systems, it is important that attention and time is devoted to the assessment of training requirements, the design of the corporate training program, the scheduling of training so that all users receive training, and an evaluation and follow-up program to address individual support needs. This will be a continual requirement if users are to advance beyond rudimentary levels of system use.

A corporate-wide training policy can also help overcome some of the problems posed by the unplanned proliferation of personal computers and software. The policy can enable a standard quality of training; avoid unnecessary or redundant training design efforts, and ensure that all users are properly trained on corporate-wide technologies, such as electronic mail, which are as strong as their weakest links.

Combining training in new workflow, process and procedures with the operation of the new system is an effective way of giving new users a context for its use. Determining which functions or tools to provide to the users first is an important decision. Often, electronic messaging is a good way to slowly introduce people to a system without adding unnecessary complexity, or changing existing procedures.

Some organizations have found that introducing one tool at a time, starting with one that is reasonably easy to learn, is an effective and non-threatening way to gently ease the user into the system and to build confidence. Hands-on learning is the most effective means of training at this point in time. However, we can envision a day (in the not too distant future) when training could be delivered to the individual at the time of need, through a combined working/learning system. Such a system would combine interactive learning with working tools to create the kind of environment where learning is part of everyday working life. There will be a great deal of learning going on as this transition takes place, and there is much to be gained by using technology to create this type of supportive environment.

Planning and Action

The bridge between planning and action is a one-year Action Plan which defines the desired short-term movement. This plan should describe the ongoing support and services to be provided within the existing systems framework, the entry pilot projects to be initiated, and the ongoing strategic planning projects and activities to be carried out during the year.

Many of these activities will require research, discussion and resolution of issues which are not as well defined as specific pilot projects. While the specific issues will vary for each enterprise, there are a number of common objectives in concluding the strategic planning effort with a one-year Action Plan:

- To ensure that the needs of users are met, within the overall framework of a long-term direction for technology.
- To provide a tactical planning tool which provides the basis for implementation of all items identified through the strategic planning process for ongoing research, evaluation, study and implementation.
- To identify the resources, both capital and human, required to implement the strategy as well as provide a means of ongoing comparison of the relative importance each is given.
- To establish a vehicle for feedback from all planning, study, implementation and research activities by means of yearly regeneration of, at very least, the Action Plan.
- To provide the basis for taking action, thereby ensuring the proper balance of planning and implementation activities is maintained for successful evolution.

There are four major steps in constructing an Action Plan.

One
Sort all action items, projects or less formal work activities into the three basic categories of action planning:

- **On-going**: Existing systems services and projects which will require human resources and capital or expenses to continue or complete.
- **Strategic Planning**: Activities and projects identified during the planning process requiring initiation, further research, monitoring or evaluation to complete.
- **Entry Pilots**: Pilot projects identified within the plan to be initiated and/or implemented during the coming year.

Two
For those items which are to be considered formal projects, detailed work plans will need to be drawn. These will define the projects:

- objectives
- deliverables

- method of work
- milestones and related activities
- schedule
- human resources and skills (user or implementor)
- budget
- roles and responsibilities
- change and completion procedures

Note that activities such as ongoing evaluation of feedback from a user committee, for example, would *not* require a formal work plan. It is, however, wise to identify such activities and to assign resources and and responsibility for their completion.

Three
Management and control methods such as critical path or PERT charts can be utilized to illustrate the overlaps in resources, projects and deliverables (the work itself). Illustrating all of the work items in this fashion can help to resolve conflicts in timing and resource allocation. The critical control points should be:

- time and schedule
- quality of deliverables
- human resources, ensuring the best distribution and utilization of skills and experience
- budget

Four
Totaling all known resources (person days, capital, expense) applied to each of the three categories and then determining the percentage of total available resource that each represents. For example, this may show that most of the available resources are already committed to ongoing activities. If such is the case, a percentage must be freed up to ensure that adequate resources are applied to complete the the planning items. It is possible to forecast how these percentages might shift over the five-year planning horizon as pilots become operational and as the planning process becomes well established.

The Action Plan

The example in Figure 13.3 indicates the types of activities that might fall into each of the three basic action planning categories. A one-year view is the most practical for tactical planning purposes in that it represents one fiscal budget planning period. Beyond a year, it is likely only possible to do a forecast, rather than a detailed action plan with individual project plans as required.

As discussed in the previous section, the Action Plan, of necessity, must be better defined in terms of specific projects, their deliverables, timetable, resources and required budget. The next task is for top management to reach an *agreement* on proceeding with the plan. Agreements will have to be made with user organizations and implementors to provide the required resources to each of the projects requiring user participation.

ACTION PLANNING ACTIVITIES/PROJECTS		
ONGOING ACTIVITIES	STRATEGIC PLANNING	ENTRY PILOTS
DDP/MIS Development ■ Financial Application ■ Personnel Information System PC Acquisition Micro Training Telephone Systems Word Processing Records Management Program	Strategic Framework ■ environmental scanning ■ technology forecast update Strategic Direction ■ reinvestment model development Technology Strategy ■ functional description ■ corporate-wide tools ■ detailed design for implementation ■ tools diffusion plan ■ information modeling in finance Analysis and Evaluation Policy ■ systems requirements ■ cost/benefit, feasibility ■ design ■ impact/refinement Technology Standards Policy Human Resource Policy Work Environment Research Project Training Methods Research	Tools Diffusion Plan 1) Pilot 'A' ■ Project Plan Development ■ Requirements Analysis ■ Design and Vendor Selection ■ Implementation 2) Pilot 'B' ■ Requirements Analysis 3) IRC (Pilot in Research) ■ Definition ■ Design ■ Implementation 4) Technology Trials ■ Computer Conferencing ■ Video Conferencing ■ Micro — MF Interface
% Resources _____ Capital Required _____ Ongoing Expenses _____	% Resources _____ Capital Required _____ Ongoing Expenses _____	% Resources _____ Capital Required _____ Ongoing Expenses _____

Figure 13.3   Action Plan

Priorities will have to be set, based on an appropriate balance of all resources against the three categories of activity to ensure that the long-term payoffs are not sacrificed for short-term ad-hoc activity. Conversely, it would be inappropriate for most organizations to curtail the majority of their current activities such as ongoing word processing, microcomputer acquisitions and records management activities, in favor of longer term planning activities, exclusively.

Balancing action and planning in appropriate proportions is often difficult and challenging. We find that many organizations simply cannot break out of the "fire fighting" syndrome, where their attention is totally focused on today's problems and issues. The deliberate allocation of time and dollars to planning and strategic projects and activities will help you bring tomorrow's desired state within the grasp of today.

This requires *working the plan* rather than *planning the work*. To work the plan there must be an underlying basic agreement that the direction the plan proposes is sound and worth working toward. The true test of this lies in the degree of senior management sponsorship in the form of actual resource commitments, and visibility of the endeavor. It is with the commitment to an Action Plan that expectations can be realistically set (if it is not in the plan, it will not likely happen this year), and legitimization of the change process can take place.

Undoubtedly, things will change throughout the year: therefore modifications of objectives may be required. The focus is not on strict adherence to "the plan", but rather on the people and their relationship to the plan.

As with any plan, the strategic systems plan has a rolling time horizon. That is, as short-term objectives are realized, the horizon of the plan rolls, requiring review and regeneration of the longer-term objectives. At certain points it may be advisable to regenerate the plan entirely. At minimum, the Strategic Framework and Strategic Direction should be revisited each year to test the assumptions, and update any invalid information. The Action Plan needs to be regenerated each year as the plan moves from a long-term to a mid-term horizon.

Evolution in Systems and Planning

Organizations mature in their use of, and planning for systems. While integrated office systems have a far-reaching and in one sense, revolutionary impact on organizations, their growth tends to be evolutionary. Consequently a planning method and process must position the organization to mature and evolve in its use of the new technologies. How can we describe the evolution of systems and systems planning? What can we learn about the past to understand where we are now and what the future can bring?

Over the years, many thinkers have developed stage theories to explain evolution and growth in a variety of areas. Freud, for example, developed a theory of psycho-sexual development. In this theory the libido, or sexual energy, moved to various parts of the body as the individual matured. A person was said to have problems if this growth was arrested at one of the stages.

Many writers and practitioners have attempted to develop theories about the "stages" of growth organizations pass through in their use of systems. The classic example of this was the work of C.F. Gibson and R.L. Nolan, who attempted to show how organizations progress through four stages from the initiation of data-processing technology through to a mature development stage.[1] In a subsequent article, Nolan expanded the theory to six stages in an attempt to explain the continual rise of EDP expense levels and new data-processing innovations.[2]

With the introduction and growth of the new office technologies, many others have jumped into the fray with various theories about how organizations mature in their use of office systems.[3]

Unfortunately, stage theories have, in general, some inherent problems. To begin, systems growth tends not to evolve in clear cut stages. Rather, growth tends to progress along a continuum. Stage theories are often somewhat forced abstractions of reality which do not take into account the subtleties of evolutionary growth.

Stage theories also tend to imply that growth is one-dimensional and that an organization matures in various areas in a uniform fashion. Unfortunately, reality is not that simple. An organization can be very advanced in its handling of one issue, such as its human resource policies on systems; at the same time it can be quite backward on other issues, such as the sophistication of its network.

Stage theorists also have the nasty habit of becoming so enamored with their theory that they can loose sight of reality, or worse, start bending reality to fit their theory.

Often then, stage theories blur rather than elucidate the problem of understanding how organizations mature in their use of systems. For these reasons we have avoided attempting to develop a new "stage theory", even though existing theories are inadequate.

Throughout the book, however, we have explained differences between "traditional" data processing, office and telephone systems on the one hand, and the product of their convergence — integrated office systems. This distinction is in no way meant to be critical or disparaging about traditional technologies. The traditional data processing systems being implemented today can be very complex sophisticated and beneficial systems, for example. Moreover, being critical of the past, is in general, a rather shortsighted undertaking. As Antoine de Saint-Exupery put it:

> We should welcome the future for soon it will be the past. But we should respect the past, for it was once all that was humanly possible.

As the technologies evolve, so do organizations as well, in their use of technology, their organizational structure, their knowledge of opportunities, and overall, the sophistication and comprehensiveness of their systems planning.

To understand this process of evolution, it is useful to summarize how the various dimensions of systems planning evolve as organizations move from these traditional to integrated technologies. By examining how organizations mature in their evolution towards fully integrated systems, you can help situate yourself and begin to formulate a plan to manage the transition. This will also enable us to project the various ways that planning will change as your organization grows into the future.

Traditional Systems and Planning

When organizations employ traditional data-processing, office and telephone technologies, planning for computers, office and telecommunications technologies tends to be somewhat separate. Systems planning and business planning also are usually somewhat separate activities, as systems are viewed primarily from the simple perspective of displacing or avoiding cost. The relationship between systems planning and implementations is relatively straightforward, as planning always precedes, or at least should preceed, an implementation.

During the era of traditional systems, the formulation of a Strategic Framework for systems planning is generally viewed to be completely outside the purview of systems planning. Similarly, there is no Strategic Direction, in the sense described in this book. Often, a plan is based on a list of applications that need to be developed and technology that needs to be acquired. Such limited plans often do not even exist for word-processing or telecommunications systems.

Workstation tools which directly support office personnel tend to be stand-alone, individual or isolated capabilities. Typical examples are a terminal which a manager uses to create a database or a stand-alone word-processing system, with a capability to use a stand-alone text messaging system. Traditional systems are also, by definition, not integrated. Integration is done by human intervention. For example, a user may take a printout from a computer database and rekey a table into a word-processing system to produce a report.

Traditional computer systems also tend to have a highly centralized architecture where a number of devices were attached directly to a main frame. With the rise of distributed data processing in the 1970s, architectures tended to become more decentralized. With the growth of word processing and microcomputers along with other independent computing devices like intelligent photocopiers, global technology architectures became, in one sense, more distributed. In another sense, however, these devices were not really part of a global technology architecture, in the same way that a stand-alone garage, doghouse, tool shed and tree house are not really part of the "architecture" of a house.

Traditional computer network architectures are "closed". That is, they are self-contained systems for one organization, enabling communication between devices and generally one vendor and using vendor proprietary architectures.

Technology policy is centered on guidelines, standards and regulations regarding how end-users can have access to computing facilities; when computing resources will be available; how systems operations will be handled; and what kind of personal computers user departments can purchase.

It is infrequent that the Human Resources manager plays a central role during this period. However, as more and more people in the organization use computer terminals or personal computers of some kind directly, this begins to change. An example is of the case the word-processing operator. The transition from being a secretary to word-processing operator affected Human Resource management in a number of ways. Jobs had to be redesigned. Often, this meant a change in the employee's classification and compensation level. Word processing had implications for career paths, for employee evaluation and monitoring and for supervision.

The proliferation of microcomputers also has generally not been viewed as raising important human resource issues. This is because personal computers implemented in an unplanned fashion, were generally not viewed as part of the overall corporate system. When a negligible portion of the overall office population was directly supported by a computer system, education and training were also often not viewed as being central challenges requiring significant resources.

The world of office space planning and design also tends to be somewhat separate from the world of systems planning. In some cases, word-processing centers have been designed to jointly optimize the technology with the physical environment. One obvious area of convergence is the design of the computer center.

Integrated Office Systems Initiation and Planning

As the enterprise initiates strategic planning for integrated office systems, organizational structures begin to change. Typically, there is the rise of ad hoc committees, task force and steering committees which attempt some coordination and, perhaps, the initiation of pilot or planning activities. This leads to the establishment of more formal organization bodies including permanent senior management committees, a formal office systems function and clear division of responsibilities for planning and implementing these systems.

The relationship between systems planning and overall business planning evolves as the organization matures in its use of technology. The two types of planning begin to merge as technology becomes an important component of achieving the overall business goals of the organization. Rather than a tactical weapon in the battle for efficiency, technology becomes a strategic weapon in winning the whole war. There is also an initial convergence in planning for computer, office and telecommunications technologies. The relationship between systems *planning* and systems *implementation* also evolves as the organization matures. Experimentation, technology trials, and entry pilots occur simultaneously with, and may actually preceed, the development of a complete integrated office systems plan. Like love and marriage, planning and implementation go together hand in hand.

During this period, there is more emphasis on understanding the strategic context or framework within which the organization finds itself as it begins to plan. As well, the plan, rather than focusing on a list of applications, should contain a Strategic Direction outlining an overall strategy on how the enterprise will use technology to achieve its business objectives. Through assessing opportunities at both the corporate and departmental levels, a projection of costs and benefits for integrated office systems can be made. The benefits tend to go beyond cost displacement, pointing to opportunities to add value to the organization's work.

Rather than stand-alone word-processing or data-processing applications, we see an initial set of corporate-wide tools such as electronic messaging implemented. As well, a limited set of tools may be implemented in an entry pilot which goes beyond the stand-alone desktop micros and, for example, links personal computers together using a local area network; providing messaging, file sharing, and scheduling capabilities. Typically, there is some degree of integration, for example, the implementation of a micro-mainframe connection, or the ability to roll up spreadsheets across departments for consolidated financial planning. However, such integration is still somewhat labor-intensive as the individual and user is required to execute commands or programs to link various facilities or tools together.

As the enterprise initiates its first pilots, the insular approach to technology architecture begins to give way to a more interfaced structure. For example, a local area network may connect microcomputers, file servers and printers with each other, while at the same time providing initial links to some corporate computing facilities. Desktop microcomputers may be interfaced to the telephone system through specialized devices on the desktop.

Although it is not possible to implement a fully open network architecture where equipment from various networks can communicate, we begin to see plans which position the organization to evolve towards such architectures. The initial plan can adopt a set of standard network protocols which enable a transitional step towards open systems.

The Information Architecture also begins to go beyond internal computerized information to build a structure for information coming from other sources. It may also make sense to go beyond the limited concept of an Information Center to the establishment of an Information Resource Center to enable the implementation of this broader approach to architecture.

We begin to see more extensive collaboration between the systems department and other stakeholders regarding policies in the areas such as technical standards, security and confidentiality, systems operations, vendor selection, and the assessment of requirements and cost justification of departmental systems.

As the new technology extends in breadth, scope, and depth, it begins to directly impact many aspects of the organization's social architecture. As a result, it makes a lot of sense to involve the Human Resource manager in the process. Critical issues where policies become necessary include job design and redesign, retraining, career planning, classification, compensation, work patterns, retirement issues and labor management-relations.

The growing extension of workstations often precipitates a rethinking of the physical environment issues both from the perspective of implementing successful pilots and also in terms of the long-range implications of technology for the physical plant. As a result, policies can be formulated to help create optimal settings within which people can work productively using technology.

A leadership strategy is now required to implement both the short-term action plan and entry pilots. This is necessary, as we have shown, to facilitate joint user-implementor ownership of this system and also to provide users with the motivation to support and participate in change. Strategies that emphasize cooperation and participation between designers and implementors on the one hand and users on the other are found to most successful. The importance of standardized education programs and training packages also becomes more visible.

The Future

How will integrated organizations evolve in their planning for and use of integrated office systems in the future? From the experience to date of those undergoing widespread implementations some directions emerging.

To begin, the organization of planning appears to evolve. The senior management team, including senior managers from line and user organizations, tend to take responsibility for corporate-wide integrated systems planning. The debates over responsibilities tend to no longer be between data-processing and administrative managers, but within management as a whole. At the same time, there is a trend towards line departments taking a more autonomous role, within the framework of corporate objectives.

Strategic business planning and systems planning converge further as the organization evolves in its objectives, goals and mission through the innovative use of new technology. The strategic business framework sets, not only the context for systems planning but the very foundation. Systems planning, in one sense becomes a part of strategic business planning. At the same time planning for data-processing, office and telecommunications systems becomes a unified process. Systems planning and implementation, rather than being parallel processes are fully iterative, with cybernetic feedback between the two. Experience drives planning and planning drives experience.

Rather than simply projecting or forecasting likely costs and benefits, these can be estimated on the basis of actual experience in evaluating system implementations. The business case for some technologies changes as they, like a telephone system, become considered a business imperative. The case focuses on the costs and benefits of various alternative systems strategies, rather than on whether or not to procede at all.

We can foresee a rich and broad range of tools integrated into workstations. These include corporate-wide technologies such as compound document (text, data, voice and image) messaging, interactive video teleconferencing, and intelligent networks providing automatic access to thousands of external databases. They will also include specialized workstation technologies in various departments, in particular expert systems which use artificial intelligence techniques to perform the work of human experts, thereby freeing humans to evolve in their creative capacities. Integration is also performed by the technology rather than by human intervention.

The Global Technology Architecture becomes fully hybrid, with desktop, workgroup, departmental, corporate and external technologies distributing computer intelligence where it is most appropriately located and owned. Rather than technologies being linked or interfaced together, we will evolve to fully integrated and compatible systems, based on public standards. Even in a multi-vendor environment (assuming that IBM does not swallow all other computer companies) such open systems will eventually prove an effective vaccine for "incompatibilitaphobia". Open systems will help enable the delivery of critical capabilities to users, and the growth and evolution of systems to potentially all people in the enterprise.

There is also a trend for technology policy in the areas discussed in this book to be jointly formulated through participation of line departments and senior management. Such policy, while clear and firmly enforced, deals with strategic issues, freeing up departments to act autonomously and innovatively in the planning for systems in their business function.

It appears that as the nature of work changes, human resource planning expertise will become more important both within the formal Human Resources department and throughout the organization. Ironically as technological innovation diffuses, people skills and knowledge become more critical, as will the ability to design, implement and evaluate the settings within which people work. The combining of technology, environment and people — a science now in its infancy — will likely bring about organizations whose performance capacities are unthinkable today.

Rather than users having a role or "participating" in the design of systems, users will become the designers. The role of the Systems function will further evolve from being owners, designers, implementors and planners of technology to also become leaders, educators, innovators, collaborators and agents of change. Just as writing skills are distributed throughout organizations, so will be expertise in customizing powerful technologies to meet productivity and quality of work life needs.

There is also a trend for systems education and training to become integrated into a job. The working-learning environment is technically feasible today. The workstation can teach the user about more than how it works. It can be a window on the world of education, not to mention a gold mine for those entering the interactive-videodisc courseware marketplace.

Finally, the short term Action Plan becomes a living, breathing document. It is continually being evaluated and adjusted in the light of experience implementing systems and policies, as well as the evolving framework and overall systems strategy.

This evolution of systems planning is summarized in Figure 14.1.

Integrated Office Systems and the New Manager

As computer, office and telecommunication technologies converge in your organization a new potential is being born. More than with any previous wave of technological innovation, the potential is arising to *support* people in their work, rather than to simply replace them, or chain them to the repetitive discipline of a machine. Rather than machine-tenders, humanity is offered the potential of evolving further as tool-users. And with this, organizations are presented with the opportunity of taking historic leaps in productivity and mission.

Such an optimistic view, however, is in contrast to the reality of many system implementations today. It is our contention that such implementations are generally based on the old views of systems and the old models of systems planning.

The desktop microcomputer is shattering these views and these models.

	Traditional	Initiation	The Future
1. PLANNING PROCESS			
Organization	-ad hoc	-formalizing	-top management ownership and autonomous user departments
Business and IOS Planning	-separate	-merging	-together
Systems Planning	-independent	-converging	-unified
Planning/Implementation	-planning first	-simultaneous	-iterative
2. STRATEGIC FRAMEWORK	-not linked to systems planning	-initial context defined	-foundation of systems planning
3. STRATEGIC DIRECTION			
Strategy	-technology plan	-coordinated planning	-unified strategy
Cost Benefit	-DP, WP cost displacement	-projection of cost/benefits	-evaluation impact -business imperative
4. WORKSTATION TOOLS	-isolated technologies	-limited set of tools	-broad range of tools
Integration	-human	-human/system	-system
5. GLOBAL TECHNOLOGY	-centralized DP	-interrelated	-multilevel -hybrid
Intelligence of the System	-insular	-interfaced	-integrated
6. NETWORK ARCHITECTURE	-closed -single vendor	-transitional	-open -any vendor
7. INFORMATION ARCHITECTURE	-for internal computerized information	-interfaced	-multilevel, multimedia external & internal
	-information center	-information resource center	-decentralized IRM
8. TECHNOLOGY POLICY	-limited policies issued	-collaboration over more extensive policies	-joint ownership between MIS & user departments
9. HUMAN RESOURCES			
Job Impact	-limited	-redesign	-evolving expertise
HR Role	-marginal HR involved	-HR manager role defined	-HR mission evolves
10. ENVIRONMENT	-environmental and systems planning are separate	-initial convergence of environmental and systems planning	-full integration of environmental and systems planning
11. IMPLEMENTATION STRATEGY			
Leadership	-systems designers — technologist	-cooperative/ participative	-user as designer
Education	-ad hoc briefings	-education program	-working/learning environment
Training	-groping	-some training packages	-self-paced/ interactive
Action Plan	-for traditional technologies	-implement first integrated office	-ongoing, iterative planning

Figure 14.1   Evolution of Systems Planning

It points to changes in the use of, and ownership of technology. It has raised the possibility of new objectives for technology. It has introduced the "human imperative" with a vengeance. It has implications for every aspect of the work system right down to the height of your desk. It has introduced technical issues that few of us dreamed of in the early years of data processing. And it is confronting every executive, every manager, every person concerned about productivity with an historic challenge.

The new technology has raised the need for a new kind of manager — a manager who sees no contradiction between productivity and the quality of work life; who can think and plan strategically; who has the courage to lead change; who has the confidence to encourage innovation; who seeks user participation and joint-ownership of problems and system solutions; and who is willing, by personal example, to integrate technology into his or her job.

In many ways, the new technology is at the center of the transformation of yesterday's managers to tomorrow's leaders. The challenge we face is to learn from the past and go forward. The stakes are high — for our organizations, for the people in them, and for ourselves.

Notes

Chapter 1
1. The *Globe and Mail*, November 14, 1983.

Chapter 2
1. *The Electronic Office in Canada*, Supply and Services Canada, May 1982.
2. John Naisbitt, *Megatrends*, Warner Books Inc., New York, 1982.
3. James Martin, World Seminar, sponsored by the Technology Transfer Institute, New York, 1980.
4. Art Benjamin, "D.P. Blood on the Office Carpet", *Computing Canada*, June 15, 1979.
5. Don Tapscott, *Office Automation: A User-Driven Method*, Plenum Press, New York, 1982.

Chapter 3
1. This formulation has become colloquial to describe data processing executives.
2. John D.C. Roach and Thomas A. Schultz, *Strategic Planning in the 1980s: Do we really need it?*, Booz-Allen & Hamilton Inc., 1982.

Chapter 5
1. Mary Baetz, *The Human Imperative: Planning for People in the Electronic Office*, Toronto, Holt, Rinehart and Winston, 1985.

Chapter 7
1. Reprinted by permission from Exxon Research and Engineering Company © 1984.
2. Martin Healy, "Junking the Mainframe", *Datamation*, Vol. 29, No. 8.
3. Peter Keen and Morton Scott, *Decision Support Systems: An Organizational Perspective*, Addison Wesley, Reading, Massachusetts, 1978.

Chapter 8
1. Reprinted by permission from *Business Systems Planning*, IBM Manual No. GE020-0527, © 1981.

2. Reprinted by permission from *Business Systems Planning*, IBM Manual No. GE020-0527, © 1981.
3. James Martin, *Strategic Data Planning Methodologies*, Prentice-Hall, New Jersey, 1982, and *An Information Systems Manifesto*, Prentice-Hall, New Jersey, 1984.
4. James Martin, *Strategic Data Planning Methodologies*, Prentice-Hall, New Jersey, 1982, and *An Information Systems Manifesto*, Prentice-Hall, New Jersey, 1984.
5. James Martin, *Strategic Data Planning Methodologies*, Prentice-Hall New Jersey, 1982, and *An Information Systems Manifesto*, Prentice-Hall, New Jersey, 1984.

Chapter 9

1. Don Tapscott, "LANs: The Hottest Topic in Office Automation", *Computing Canada*, Vol. 8, No. 18, 1982.

Chapter 11

1. Judith Gregory, "Race Against Time", *Office: Technology and People*, 1982.
2. Shoshanah Zuboff, "Computer-Mediated Work: The Emerging Challenge", a response to "Race Against Time", *Office: Technology and People*, 1982.

Chapter 12

1. Elaine Cohen and Aaron Cohen, *Planning the Electronic Office*, McGraw-Hill, New York, 1983.
2. January 1979 issue of *Contract*.

Chapter 14

1. C.F. Gibson and R.L. Nolan, "Managing the Four Stages of EDP Growth", *Harvard Business Review*, January-February 1974.
2. R.L. Nolan, "Managing the Crisis in Data Processing", *Harvard Business Review*, March-April 1979, pp. 115-26.
3. Robert I. Baxter, and George F. Krall, "Six Stages Toward the Automated Office", *Words*, October-November 1979, pp. 20-24.
4. Christopher J. Burns, "The Evolution of Office Information Systems", *Datamation*, April 1977.
5. Larry Day, Stages of Growth in Office Automation, presentation to the Diebold Office Automation Program, 1980.
6. F.W. Holmes, "IRM — Organizing for the Office of the Future", *Journal of Systems Management*, 1979.
7. M.A. Lieberman, J.S. Selig and J.J. Walsh, *Office Automation, A Manager's Guide For Improved Productivity*, Wiley, New York, 1982.

8. N. Dean Meyer, "Stages of Growth: Preparing Users for Automation", *Data Training*, Vol. 1, No. 10, September 1982.

9. N. Dean Meyer, "Don't Plan", *Computerworld OA*, February 23, 1983.

10. P.A. Strassman, "Stages of Growth", *Datamation*, October 1976.

11. Michael D. Zisman, "Office Automation: Revolution or Evolution", *Sloan Management Review*, Spring 1978, pp. 1–16.

Selected Sources

Amara, Roy, and Andrew J. Lipinski, *Business Planning for an Uncertain Future*, Pergamon Press, New York 1983.

American Federation of Information Processing Societies, 1983 Office Automation Conference Digest, Los Angeles, California, February 21–23, 1983.

American Federation of Information Processing Societies, 1984 Office Automation Conference Digest, Philadelphia, Pennsylvania, February 21–23, 1984.

American Productivity Center, White-Collar Productivity: The National Challenge, Sponsored by Steelcase Inc., 1982.

Ansoff, Igor H., *Strategic Management*, Macmillan, London and Basingstoke 1979.

Arthur D. Little Service, "The U.S. Office Automation Market, 1983–1988: The Evolution Toward Integrated Information Processing," *Impact*, July 1983.

Asner, Michael, *Up Your Computer*, Marchmount Publishing, Toronto 1983.

Bair, James H., "Communications in the Office of the Future: Where the Real Payoff May Be", *Business Communications Review*, January-February 1979.

——, "Era", presented to the *Financial Times of London* Conference on The Electronic Office: Threshold of a New Era.

Bair, James H., and Mary J. Culman, "Strategy: Where Do You Start?", *Management Technology*, July 1983.

——, "The Potential Impact of Office Automation," *Journal of the American Society for Information Science*, Vol. 34, No. 3, 1983.

Bair, James H., and Kathryn J. Nelson, "User Needs as a Basis of Systems Planning", *Advances in Office Automation*, Wiley, Heyden Ltd 1984.

——, User Needs as the Basis of Strategic Planning, Bell Northern Research, Inc. and Los Alamos National Laboratory, March 1983.

Baxter, Robert I., and George F. Krall, "Six Stages Toward the Automated Office", *Words*, October-November 1979, pp. 20–24.

Bennett, John, Donald Case, Jon Sandelin, and Michael Smith (Eds.), *Visual Display Terminals, Usability Issues and Health Concerns,* Prentice-Hall, New Jersey 1984.

Booth, Grayce M., *The Design of Complex Information Systems*, McGraw-Hill Book Company, New York 1983.

Burns, Christopher J., "The Evolution of Office Information Systems", *Datamation*, April 1977.

Business Week, "Computer Shock Hits the Office", August 1983, pp. 46–49.

Carlisle, J.H., "The Automated Office: Making It Productive for Tomorrow's Manager", *Administrative Management*, January 1981.

Caswell, Stephen A., "Strategic Planning: What it Really Means", *Computerworld Canada*, July 13, 1984, p. 25.

Chang, Shi-Kuo (Ed.), *Management and Office Information Systems*, Plenum Press, New York 1984.

Chorafas, Dimitris N., *Office Automation: The Productivity Challenge*, Prentice-Hall, New Jersey 1982.

Connell, J.J., "The 'People Factor' In the Office of the Future", *Administrative Management*, January 1980.

Davies, Donald W., and Derek L.A. Barber, *Communications Networks for Computers*, Wiley, New York 1977.

Davis, Stanley M., "Transforming Organizations: The Key to Strategy Is Context", *Organizational Dynamics*, Winter 1982, pp. 64–75.

Derfler, Frank Jr., *A Manager's Guide to Local Networks*, Prentice-Hall, New Jersey 1983.

DeSousa, M.R., "Electronic Information Interchange in an Office Environment", *IBM Systems Journal*, 1981, pp. 4–22.

Diebold Group Inc., "People Impacts of Office Technology: The Socio-Technical Approach", The Diebold Automated Office Program, May 1982.

———. "Developing an Office Automation Plan", The Diebold Automated Office Program, December 1980.

Dixon, R.C., N.C. Strole and J.D. Markov, "A Token-Ring Network for Local Data Communications", *IBM Systems Journal*, 1983, pp. 47–62.

Driscoll, James W., "How to Humanize Office Automation", *Office: Technology and People*, 1982, pp. 167–76.

Englebart, D.C. *Augmenting Human Intellect: A Conceptual Framework*, Project No. 3578, Menlo Park, California, Stanford Research Institute, October 1962.

Evered, Roger, "So What *is* Strategy?" *Long Range Planning*, 1983, pp. 57–72.

Exxon Research and Engineering Company, "Corporate Services' Plan for Automated Information, Office and Computing Systems", Florham Park, New Jersey 1981.

Franklin Research Center, "Office of the Future Planning Model", *OPTIMUS*, June 1, 1982.

Fullerton, R.W., "Office Automation, Personnel and the New Technology", *Personnel Journal*, October 1980, pp. 815–20.

Galitz, W.O., *Guidelines for Achieving Clarity in Screen Format Design*, CNA, Chicago, September 1979.

Gluck, Frederick W., Stephen P. Kaufman, and A. Steven Walleck, "Strategic Management for Competitive Advantage", *Strategic Management*, July-August 1980, pp. 154–61.

———, "The Four Phases of Strategic Management", *The Journal of Business Strategy*, pp. 9–21.

Goldman, Michael E., "A Plan That Worked", *Computerworld OA*.

Green, Paul E. Jr. (Ed.), "The Structure of Computer Networks", *Computer Networks, Architectures and Protocols*, Plenum Press, New York 1982.

Gregory, Judith, "Race Against Time", *Office: Technology and People*, 1982.

Hammer, Michael, "A Progress Report on Office Automation: The Need for Integration", *ICP Interface Administrative and Accounting*, Summer 1982.

Hammer, M. and M.D. Zisman, Design and Implementation of Office Information Systems, *Office Automation: Invited Papers, Infotech State of the Art Report*, Infotech Ltd., Maidenhead, Berkshire, England, Series 8, No. 3, 1980.

Hiltz, S.R., and M. Turoof, *The Network Nation*, Addison Wesley, Reading, Massachusetts, 1978.

Holmes, F.W., "IRM — Organizing for the Office of the Future", *Journal of Systems Management*, 1979.

IBM, *Business Systems Planning, Information Systems Planning Guide*, Third Edition, July, 1983.

IBM, *Office Systems Planning, Customer Guide*, GE20-0527-3. November 1981.

IEEE, Proceedings of, Special Issue on OSI — Standard Architecture and Protocols, Annual Index, Vol. 71, No. 12, 1983.

International Data Corporation, *Organizational Strategies For Office Automation*, a research report prepared for IDC continuous information services clients, April 1982.

Irving, Ric, *Planning For Office Automation*, Microtel 1984.

Jarvis, William F., "Managing Your Way Around Option Shock", *Canadian Office*, August 1983.

———, "The New Challenges of Management Support Systems", *Computer Data*, April 1983.

Johansen, R., et al., *Electronic Meetings*, Addison Wesley, Reading, Massachusetts, 1979.

Judson, Arnold S., "The Awkward Truth About Productivity", *Harvard Business Review*, September-October 1982, pp. 93-97.

Kearns, David T., Keynote Address, 1984 Office Automation Conference, Xerox Corporation, Los Angeles, February 20, 1984.

Keen, P.G.W., and Morton, Scott, *Decision Support Systems: An Organizational Perspective*, Addison Wesley, Reading, Massachusetts, 1978.

Landau, Robert, James H. Bair and Jean J. Siegman, *Emerging Office Systems*, Ablex Publishing Company, New Jersey 1982.

Lieberman, Mark A., J. Selig and John J. Walsh, *Office Automation, A Manager's Guide for Improved Productivity*, Wiley, New York 1982.

Lodahl, Thomas M., "Micro-Power For Managers", *Management Technology*, August 1983.

———, "Planning During a Recession: Start Now", *Computerworld OA*, December 1982.

Mallia, Anthony J., "Who Should Manage Office Technology?", *Management Technology*, August 1983, pp. 44-47.

Margulies, Newton, and Lora Colflesh, "A Socio-Technical Approach to Planning and Implementing New Technology", *Training and Development Journal*, December 1982, pp. 16-29.

Martin, James, *An Information Systems Manifesto*, Prentice-Hall, New Jersey 1984.

———, *Application Development Without Programmers*, Prentice-Hall, New Jersey 1982.

———, *Managing the Data-Base Environment*, Prentice-Hall, New Jersey 1983.

———, *Strategic Data-Planning Methodologies*, Prentice-Hall, New Jersey 1982.

McFarlan, F. Warren, "Information Technology Changes the Way You Compete", *Harvard Business Review*, May-June 1984, pp. 98-103.

McKenney, James L., and F. Warren McFarlan, "The Information Archipelago — Maps and Bridges", *Harvard Business Review*, September-October 1982, pp. 109-19.

Meyer, N. Dean, "Building a Winning Team", *Today's Office*, 1983, pp. 40-51.

———, "Don't Plan", *Computerworld OA*, February 23, 1983.

———, "Planning for Integration In Office Automation", *Electronic Office: Management and Technology*, Auerbach, 1980.

————, "Stages of Growth: Preparing Users for Automation", *Data Training*, September 1982.

Meyer, N.D., and T.M. Lodahl, "Six Pathways to Office Automation", *Administrative Management*, March 1980.

NBS Special Publication 500-72, "Guidance on Requirements Analysis for Office Automation Systems", *Computer Science and Technology*, Washington, D.C., 1980.

Naffah, Najah, *Integrated Office Systems — Burotics*, North-Holland Publishing, Amsterdam 1980.

Nystom, P.C., and W.H. Starbuck (Eds.), "Remodeling Organizations and Their Environments", *Handbook of Organizational Design*, Oxford University Press, 1981.

O'Connell, Daniel J., "Strategic Planning. How To Get There From Here.", *Computerworld OA*, pp. 21-23.

Ohmae, Kenichi, *The Mind of the Strategist*, McGraw-Hill, New York 1982.

PIMS Program, "Management Productivity and Information Technology", The Strategic Planning Institute, results and conclusions from the pilot program, 1984.

Pava, Cal, *Managing Office Technology*, The Free Press, New York 1984.

Porter, Michael E., *Competitive Strategy: Techniques for Analyzing Industries and Competitors*, The Free Press, New York 1980.

Rice, Ronald E. and Associates, *The New Media, Communications, Resources and Technology*, Sage Publications, Beverly Hills 1984.

Roberts, Edward B., and Alan R. Fusfeld, "Staffing the Innovative Technology-Based Organization", *Sloan Management Review*, Spring 1981, pp. 1-34.

Rockart, John F., "The Changing Role of the Information Systems Executive: A Critical Success Factors Perspective", Massachusetts Institute of Technology, 185-19.

Rohlfs, Sabine, "User Interfaces: Environmental Considerations", *Electronic Office: Management and Technology*, Auerbach, 1980.

Rosenbaum, Linda, *Health Effects of Video Display Terminals: The Nonradiation Problems*, Health Advocacy Unit, Toronto, Department of Public Health, April 1981.

Schlefer, Jonathan, "Office Automation and Bureaucracy", *Technology Review*, July 1983, pp. 32-40.

Shah, Bharat, a working paper entitled *Perspectives on the Value of Information*.

Skilling, Johanna, "Office Technology Task Force Team Planning for the Integrated Electronic Office", *High Technology*, April 1983, pp. 69-81.

Strassman, Paul A., "Stages of Growth", *Datamation*, October 1976.

————, "Information Is Not a Manageable Resource", reprinted in *Office Technology Research Group: Overview*, Office Technology Research Group, Pasadena, California, pp. 1-9.

————, *Information Payoff: The Transformation of Work in the Electronic Age*, Macmillan, New York 1984.

Tapscott, Don, *Office Automation — A User-Driven Method*, Plenum, New York 1982.

————, "Investigating the Electronic Office", *Datamation*, March 1982, pp. 130-38.

Uhlig, Ronald P., David J. Farber and James H. Bair, *The Office of the Future*, North-Holland Publishing, Amsterdam 1979.

Ward, P.J. and Associates, "Strategic Systems Planning", *NOW*, 64th Edition, February-March 1984.

Working Women, *Race Against Time: Automation of the Office*, National Association of Office Workers, April 1980, pp. 1-31.

Zaleznik, Abraham, "Managers and Leaders: Are They Different?", *Harvard Business Review*, May-June 1977, pp. 67-78.

Zisman, Michael D., "Office Automation: Revolution or Evolution", *Sloan Management Review*, Spring 1978, pp. 1-16.

Zuboff, Shoshanah, "Computer-Mediated Work: The Emerging Challenge", a response to "Race Against Time", *Office: Technology and People*, 1982.

Index

DATE DUE

MAY 20-87			
MAY 20-87			
APR 20 1987			
NOV 1 5 1987			
DEC 1 5 1990			

HIGH SMITH REORDER #45-230